I0528107

The Wolf's Edge
Strategies for Intelligent Living

Adapt, Lead, and Thrive in Life and Work Like a Wolf

ELLEN SEDGE

Impisi™ Media LLC
Smart Work-Life Series

The Wolf's Edge

Strategies for Intelligent Living

ELLEN SEDGE

The Wolf's Edge - Strategies for Intelligent Living: Adapt, Lead, and Thrive in Life and Work Like a Wolf

Copyright © 2024 by Impisi Media

All rights reserved. No part of this publication may be reproduced, distributed, or transmitted in any form or by any means, including photocopying, recording, or other electronic or mechanical methods, without the prior written permission of the publisher, except in the case of brief quotations embodied in critical reviews and certain other noncommercial uses permitted by copyright law.

ISBN: 978-1-965722-07-7 (eBook)
ISBN: 978-1-965722-08-4 (Paperback)
ISBN: 978-1-965722-14-5 (Hardcover)

The case studies in this book are based on real-life experiences. To protect privacy, names, locations, and identifying details have been changed or omitted. Any resemblance to persons, businesses, or places beyond the intended examples is coincidental. The lessons and insights are genuine and provide practical guidance to readers on their entrepreneurial journey.

Book design by Ciska Venter.
Images by Jeanne Michelle Smith.

First printing edition 2024.

Published by Impisi™ Media LLC in the United States of America.
5830 E 2ND ST, STE 7000, CASPER, WY 82609
+1 (307) 275 8745
www.impisimedia.com
Impisi™ is subject to a trademark application by Impisi Media LLC.

Contents

Also by the Publisher

Small Business Series

Should You Start a Business or Not?
Business Entry: Starting vs Buying
3 Keys to Maximize Profitability

Smart Work-Life Series

Mastering Time for Productivity
The Wolf's Edge: Strategies for Intelligent Living
Reset with Intermittent Fasting

Click or scan the QR code to receive updates on new releases and book resources.

"The wolf is a symbol of freedom, independence, and the wild." – Unknown

This quote captures the essence of self-reliance, resilience, and authenticity. Embracing these qualities, a person can navigate life with confidence and adaptability, taking bold steps toward personal and professional goals. By fostering independence and staying true to oneself, one can thrive in challenging environments and build meaningful, impactful connections.

Introduction: The Wolf's Wisdom

*"The wolf's life is a lesson in survival, a testament to the
strength of the human spirit." - Jack London*

A Wolf's Beginning

In the stillness of the early dawn, the air carried a crisp bite as
it settled over the valley. Beneath the shadow of a towering
mountain, the land seemed to stretch on forever—untamed, wild,
and full of life. Deep within a rocky den, hidden from the vastness
outside, the alpha female had just given birth to a new generation
of the pack. The atmosphere was electric, filled with the subtle
energy of new beginnings and the ancient rhythms of survival.

Among the pups, nestled against his mother's warmth, lay Thorne, a small, silvery wolf pup. His eyes were still closed, but even in those first moments, something about him was different. He was quiet, observant in his movements, and in the way his tiny body settled against his siblings, there was an air of purpose. The other pups wriggled and squirmed, full of noisy hunger, but Thorne seemed more thoughtful, as if he were absorbing the world before he had even seen it.

Outside the den, the wind howled through the trees, carrying with it the sounds of the pack. They were out there—his future, his world. Yet for now, Thorne lay safe in the darkness, his world limited to the immediate warmth of his family. The mountain, the forest, the pack—these would all come in time. But like any journey, it had to begin with the smallest of steps. And for Thorne, that first step was simply being born into the life of a wolf.

The days passed slowly. Inside the den, there was little light, and time itself seemed to move differently. Thorne and his siblings grew stronger, nourished by their mother's milk and kept safe by the protective vigilance of the alpha male, their father. Soon, a momentous change occurred. Thorne's eyes, closed since birth, began to flutter open. The world flooded in, slowly at first, then all at once. The den, once a dark, familiar cocoon, became a place of shapes and shadows, filled with new sensations to be explored.

Thorne blinked against the dim light, his mind taking in the enormity of what lay beyond. For a moment, he lay still, staring out toward the entrance of the den where the light danced just beyond his reach. There was an entire world out there, waiting to be explored. His first steps were tentative, cautious, as he moved toward the light. Every new sight and sound filled him with awe. The rustle of leaves in the wind, the distant call of a raven, and the sound of the pack moving in the forest all hinted at the life awaiting him. His senses sharpened with each new day, his mind eagerly cataloging the lessons around him, though he had not yet ventured far from the den. The outside world fascinated him, and his curiosity grew, urging him to understand his place within it.

A Journey of Learning

Yet, despite this curiosity, Thorne was not reckless. Like the other pups, he learned to rely on the safety and wisdom of the pack. Venturing too far too quickly could mean danger. There were lessons to learn before he could take on the world outside. Each wolf had a role within the pack's carefully maintained structure. The alpha male led with strength, confidence, and clarity, while the others played their parts, from hunting to guarding the den. Thorne watched closely, absorbing these dynamics even at such an early age.

As the days turned into weeks, Thorne began to venture further from the den, accompanied by his siblings and under the watchful eyes of the older wolves. The outside world was far larger than he had imagined. It was filled with new challenges and opportunities. He stumbled at first, still learning to balance his instincts with the lessons passed down by the pack. But with each stumble came growth, and soon, Thorne's steps became more sure-footed. He was beginning to understand what it meant to be part of something larger than himself—a team that thrived together or fell apart in isolation.

Thorne's journey mirrors the path we all walk in our own lives, whether in business, family, or personal growth. Just as Thorne learned to balance his individual curiosity with the safety and structure of the pack, we too must find that delicate balance between independence and collaboration. This is one of the core lessons that wolves teach us. Success, whether in the wilderness or in the workplace, is not achieved in isolation. It is the result of teamwork, of understanding one's role within a larger system and working in harmony with others to achieve a common goal.

The wolf pack thrives because every member understands their place and contributes to the collective success of the group. The alpha leads with authority, but their authority is earned through respect, not through force. They are strong, yes, but they are also wise. They know when to lead from the front and when to step back and allow others to shine. In many ways, the role of the alpha mirrors the role of a leader in any organization. Effective leadership is not about micromanaging or demanding obedience; it is about empowering others, fostering collaboration, and guiding the team toward a shared vision.

As Thorne's eyes opened to the world around him, his understanding of his place within the pack also deepened. He began to see the connections between the wolves—the way they communicated, the way they worked together to achieve a common purpose. The howling of the wolves, for example, was not just noise; it was a form of communication, a way of maintaining unity within the pack. Each wolf's voice was unique, and together, their howls created a symphony that signaled their presence to the world.

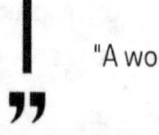 "A wolf alone can be killed, but a pack will survive"

This unity of purpose, this sense of belonging to something greater than oneself, is a lesson that applies to all aspects of life. Whether we are leading a team in a corporate setting, managing a household, or navigating personal relationships, the principles of leadership, communication, and collaboration are the same. We thrive when we work together, when we understand our roles and responsibilities, and when we communicate effectively with those around us.

But the lessons of the wolf pack go beyond teamwork and leadership. Wolves are also masters of adaptability. In the wild, conditions are constantly changing. A wolf pack must adapt to its environment, learning to hunt in different terrains, adjusting to the shifting seasons, and facing new challenges with resilience and resourcefulness. Thorne, like all wolves, had to learn these lessons from an early age. The wilderness was unforgiving, and only those who could adapt would survive.

In our own lives, adaptability is just as crucial. The business landscape is constantly evolving, and so too are the demands of our personal lives. Whether it's a sudden shift in market conditions or an unexpected challenge in our personal relationships, we must learn to adapt, to pivot when necessary, and to face new challenges with resilience. The wolf's ability to thrive in changing environments is a powerful metaphor for the adaptability and resilience we must cultivate in our own lives.

Wolf Metaphors

This book, *The Wolf's Edge: Strategies for Intelligent Living*, uses the life and behaviors of wolves as metaphors for leadership, teamwork, and personal development. It is not just a guide for thriving in the workplace; it is a blueprint for living a balanced, fulfilling life. By examining the qualities that make wolves such successful pack animals, we can uncover powerful lessons about how to lead, collaborate, and grow—both personally and professionally.

Throughout this book, you will follow Thorne's journey from a curious pup to a confident leader of his pack. Along the way, you will discover insights into leadership, communication, adaptability, and resilience that can be applied to your own life. Whether you are leading a team at work, managing relationships at home, or simply seeking personal growth, the lessons of the wolf pack offer a timeless guide to navigating the complexities of modern life.

As you journey through the book, you will be encouraged to reflect on your own life—your leadership style, your communication habits, and your approach to managing challenges. Each chapter will offer practical insights and actionable advice, helping you to navigate the complexities of modern life with the wisdom of the wolf. The aim is not just to teach you how to survive, but to show you how to thrive—how to harness your own inner strength, adapt to change, and lead with clarity and purpose.

Just as Thorne will grow to become a leader in his pack, you too can develop the skills and mindset needed to succeed in your own life. Whether it's in the boardroom or the living room, the lessons you'll learn from the wolves will help you lead with intelligence, empathy, and resilience.

Metaphor Lessons

This book offers a unique lens on leadership, teamwork, and personal growth by drawing on the behaviors of wolves. Each chapter introduces key lessons rooted in the way wolves navigate the wild. From their leadership structure to their resourcefulness, wolves embody qualities that are essential in business and personal life. The following sections provide a guide to what you can expect, offering you the tools to adapt and thrive.

We begin with leadership, hierarchy, and teamwork. Wolves thrive in an organized structure where every member knows their role.

The alpha leads with authority but also ensures the pack functions as a unit. Effective leaders know when to step up and when to let others lead. They create an environment where collaboration is as important as direction. Through wolf pack behavior, you'll explore how leadership and teamwork are interconnected and essential for success in both professional and personal realms.

Next, we dive into adaptability, resilience, and resourcefulness. Life in the wild demands constant adjustment to changing conditions. Wolves survive harsh winters, navigate scarce resources, and quickly adapt to new territories. You will discover how these traits apply to the modern world, especially when faced with challenges at work or home. This book will guide you through stories of personal and business resilience, offering insights on how to stay resourceful and adaptable in unpredictable circumstances.

Communication and social bonds are also vital in wolf packs. Their survival hinges on clear and timely communication, not just through howls but also through body language and subtle cues. Strong social bonds keep the pack united. Similarly, in life, communication is the cornerstone of successful relationships—whether in a corporate team, a family, or a social circle. In this section, you will learn strategies for fostering clear communication and building strong, trust-based relationships that strengthen your connections.

Balancing independence and collaboration is another key element. Wolves often venture out alone to explore, but they always return to the safety of the pack. This mirrors the balance between pursuing individual goals and collaborating with others. In business and personal life, finding this balance is crucial. You'll be encouraged to reflect on how you handle this duality—how you can maintain your independence while still contributing to a larger team or family unit.

Energy management, focus, and risk assessment are essential survival tools for wolves, and they are equally important for us. Wolves conserve their energy during hunts and carefully assess risks before making decisions. Similarly, managing your energy and focusing on high-priority tasks are critical for avoiding burnout. This section will offer you practical tips on staying focused, assessing risks, and making informed decisions that benefit both your personal and professional life.

The book also includes real-life case studies and examples, offering a practical connection to the concepts presented. These case studies provide insights into how leaders, professionals, and individuals have applied the wolf-inspired lessons to navigate challenges and achieve success. These examples will help ground the metaphors in everyday life, making them applicable to your own journey.

Finally, reflective exercises will allow you to engage with the material on a personal level. After each chapter, you'll be invited to reflect on your own experiences—whether it's assessing your leadership style or evaluating your communication skills. These exercises are designed to help you apply the lessons from the book directly to your life, ensuring that the knowledge gained is not just theoretical but also actionable.

This book includes exclusive downloadable resources, detailed in the Appendices. To access them, visit www.impisimedia.com/resources. You'll need to register for a free account and enter the access code found in **Appendix A** to unlock the materials.

Chapter 1

The Pack Mentality – Leadership, Hierarchy, and Teamwork

"I woke up one morning thinking about wolves and realized that wolf packs function as families. Everyone has a role, and if you act within the parameters of your role, the whole pack succeeds, and when that falls apart, so does the pack" – Jodi Picoult

Thorne Finds His Place

As the early morning light filtered into the den, Thorne's world continued to expand. His legs grew stronger, his senses sharper, and his curiosity deeper. Though he had not yet ventured far beyond the protective boundaries of the den, he could now see and hear the world much more precisely than before. The pack was always nearby, an unbreakable presence that surrounded him. Their howls echoed in the distance, their movements were purposeful, and each wolf seemed to have a role. The den that had once been a quiet sanctuary now bustled with activity, and Thorne was eager to learn more about the life that lay ahead.

Thorne began to observe the pack with a new level of awareness. The alpha, a large and formidable wolf, was always present, though not always in the front. He led with confidence, but it wasn't his size or strength that commanded attention. It was something else—something Thorne could not yet name but instinctively respected. The alpha moved through the pack with quiet authority, never needing to force his will. The other wolves deferred to him, but they did so out of respect rather than fear. This puzzled Thorne at first. He had expected leadership to be about strength, but the alpha's leadership was about something more profound: wisdom and understanding.

Thorne's place in the pack was still undefined. As the youngest, he spent most of his time with the other pups, playing and learning the first lessons of wolf life. His mother, the alpha female, was never far away, watching over him and his siblings. It was she who taught them the first lessons of teamwork. One day, as the sun began to set and the chill of the evening crept in, Thorne saw something that would stay with him. The hunting party returned, and though he had not been with them, he understood the significance of the moment. The pack had worked together, each member playing a role, and now they shared the fruits of their labor.

After the hunt, the wolves who had stayed behind to guard the den and care for the pups gathered near the hunters. Thorne watched as the adult wolves, with their bellies full, began to regurgitate partially digested food. This was a strange sight to him at first, but it soon became apparent that this act of sharing was vital for the pack's survival. The regurgitated food was meant for the pups and other wolves that had remained behind. Thorne, eager and hungry, joined the other pups as they were fed in this manner. Although he had not been part of the hunt, he was still included in the meal. This ritual not only ensured that every wolf was fed but also reinforced the bond between the hunters and the rest of the pack.

Through this experience, Thorne began to understand the pack's structure more clearly. The alpha male and female were the undisputed leaders, but they didn't lead through aggression or dominance. Instead, they set an example. They coordinated the hunts, ensured the safety of the den, and, most importantly, maintained the unity of the pack. Thorne's respect for the alpha grew, not because of his physical strength, but because of his ability to bring the pack together. Leadership, Thorne realized, was about more than just giving orders. It was about ensuring the well-being of every pack member and guiding them toward a common goal.

Thorne's learning didn't stop with observing the alpha. The more time he spent in the pack's company, the more he noticed the subtle ways in which hierarchy worked. There was a clear pecking order, but it wasn't rigid or oppressive. It was fluid, and each wolf knew its place. The older wolves, who had served the pack for years, were treated with respect, even if they no longer led hunts. The younger wolves, full of energy and ambition, were eager to prove themselves, but they also understood that their time would come. It was a balance between tradition and progression, and Thorne found comfort in knowing that his place, though small now, would evolve as he grew.

Teamwork was another lesson Thorne began to absorb, even though he wasn't old enough to join the hunts. There were other duties within the pack that were equally important. Some wolves stayed behind to guard the den while others babysat the pups. Thorne observed how these wolves took their roles seriously, ensuring the safety of the pack's future generations. They stood vigilant at the entrance to the den; their ears perked for any signs of danger. Thorne watched in admiration as they fulfilled their responsibilities with quiet dedication. This was his first real exposure to the concept of teamwork—each wolf had a role, and every role was critical to the survival of the pack.

> "For the strength of the Pack is the Wolf, and the strength of the Wolf is the Pack" – Rudyard Kipling

There were also moments of play and rest, but these, too, were part of the pack's structure. Thorne noticed how even playtime served a purpose. The pups were learning how to interact with one another, testing boundaries, and practicing the skills they would need as adults. It was during these times that Thorne began to understand the importance of communication within the pack. A quick nip from an older wolf wasn't just an act of aggression; it was a lesson in boundaries. A playful tackle from a sibling was a way to strengthen bonds. Communication wasn't just about howling or barking; it was in the small, everyday interactions that defined the relationships within the pack.

Through these experiences, Thorne's understanding of leadership, hierarchy, and teamwork deepened. It was about understanding the needs of the pack, leading by example, and knowing when to step back and let others take charge. The alpha male didn't need to control every aspect of pack life. He trusted the other wolves to fulfill their roles, just as they trusted him to guide them in times of need.

In these early days, Thorne learned that every member of the pack had a place and a purpose. Whether it was the alpha leading a hunt, a guard wolf watching over the den, or a pup learning through play, each role was essential. The pack thrived because of its unity and the respect each wolf had for the others. Thorne was still young, but he had already begun to find his place within this complex, interconnected system. The lessons of leadership, hierarchy, and teamwork would stay with him as he grew, shaping the wolf he would become.

Wolf Lessons in Business

Thorne's experiences in understanding pack hierarchy and leadership offer valuable insights that can be directly applied to the world of business. In a wolf pack, leadership is not about dominance or micromanagement; it is about guiding the team toward a common goal while respecting each member's role.

The alpha wolf leads by example, showing confidence, resilience, and strategic thinking. Business leaders can learn from this approach, especially in managing teams and organizations.

One key lesson from the wolf pack is the importance of clear roles and responsibilities. In business, each team member should know their place and understand what is expected of them. A well-functioning team, like a wolf pack, thrives on the understanding that every role contributes to overall success.

Just as the pack depends on the alpha for direction but trusts each wolf to fulfill its duties, a business should empower employees to take ownership of their tasks while ensuring alignment with the company's vision. Influential leaders recognize that micromanaging stifles creativity and innovation, just as overly controlling alphas weaken the pack.

Another crucial lesson is the value of teamwork and collaboration. Wolves depend on each other for survival; no single wolf can thrive on its own. Similarly, in business, collaboration is key to success. A company that fosters a collaborative environment encourages innovation and problem-solving. Each department, whether it be marketing, sales, or operations, has a distinct role, but its efforts must align to achieve the organization's broader goals. When departments function like isolated individuals, the business suffers. By encouraging cross-departmental teamwork, business leaders can foster a sense of unity, much like the wolves who support one another during hunts or guard duties.

Leadership in business, like in the wolf pack, also involves strategic resource allocation. The alpha ensures that food is shared among all pack members, even those who did not take part in the hunt. In business, this translates to ensuring that all resources—whether they be financial, human, or technological—are used wisely and fairly. Leaders must make decisions that balance immediate needs with long-term sustainability, just as the alpha considers the survival of the entire pack. Resource allocation should not favor one department or group over others but should be used to support the company's mission.

Lastly, effective business leadership is about building trust. In the wolf pack, trust is essential for survival. The alpha must trust the other wolves to fulfill their roles, while the pack trusts the alpha to guide them. In business, this translates to fostering an environment of trust between leaders and their teams. Employees who feel trusted are more likely to take the initiative, be creative, and feel a sense of loyalty to the organization. Trust also helps build resilience within the team, as members are more likely to support each other in times of crisis, much like wolves do when facing external threats.

Wolf Lessons in Family Life

The lessons from wolf packs also offer valuable insights into how we navigate our personal and family lives. Just as in a business setting, the dynamics within a family rely on clear roles, effective communication, and mutual trust. The leadership shown by the alpha wolf mirrors the role of a parent or guardian in a family unit. Parenting, like leading a wolf pack, requires balancing authority with empathy, ensuring that every family member feels valued and understood.

One of the most essential lessons from the wolf pack is the significance of teamwork in family life. In a pack, wolves work together to protect and provide for one another. Similarly, in a family, members must work as a team to keep harmony and meet collective needs. When parents work together to manage household responsibilities and involve their children in age-appropriate tasks, it fosters a sense of unity and shared purpose. Much like the wolves who take turns guarding the den or hunting, families function best when responsibilities are shared and each member contributes to the household's well-being.

Effective communication, another cornerstone of wolf pack life, is just as essential in a family. Wolves use body language, vocalizations, and subtle cues to maintain order and strengthen social bonds. In family life, clear and open communication is critical for resolving conflicts, expressing needs, and building strong relationships. Whether it's through a family discussion around the dinner table or a private conversation between siblings, open lines of communication help maintain the emotional health of the family. Just as wolves maintain harmony through howls and body language, families that communicate well are more resilient and able to navigate challenges.

Another wolf lesson that applies to family life is the importance of nurturing and caregiving. In a wolf pack, older members and non-breeding wolves often take on caregiving roles, such as babysitting the pups or guarding the den. This sense of collective responsibility ensures the survival of the younger generation. In a family, this can be seen in the way older siblings care for younger ones or how extended family members help support each other. The idea that it takes a village to raise a child resonates deeply with wolf pack dynamics, where survival depends on the group's ability to work together to nurture its young.

Finally, the concept of hierarchy in a wolf pack can also be applied to family life. In a healthy family dynamic, parents or guardians provide guidance and set boundaries, similar to how the alpha leads the pack. However, like the alpha wolf, effective leadership in the family is not about control or domination. It's about setting an example, making fair decisions, and ensuring that every family member feels safe and supported.

As children grow older, their roles within the family shift, much like young wolves gradually taking on more responsibilities within the pack. This evolving hierarchy allows for personal growth while maintaining the stability of the family unit.

Case Study: Aligning Leadership and Culture for Business Success

Garth was a dedicated CEO of a growing financial services company. His work ethic was unmatched, and his knowledge of the industry was extensive. Under his leadership, the company began to see rapid growth, bringing in new clients and expanding its services.

However, with this success came new challenges. Garth started noticing something unsettling: only some employees seemed to understand where the company was heading. They were completing their tasks, but there needed to be a clear sense of shared purpose. Even more concerning was the realization that his management team, the very leaders he depended on to carry out his vision, was not fully aligned with the company's goals.

This was a turning point for Garth. As the leader of the company, he realized that the organization resembled a wolf pack in many ways. For the pack to thrive, every member had to understand their role and contribute to the collective goal. Leadership wasn't just about setting direction; it was about ensuring that everyone was moving toward the same destination. In Garth's case, that destination was the long-term growth and success of the company. But how could he expect his employees to be aligned if they didn't fully understand the vision?

It became clear to Garth that leadership was more than simply making decisions and overseeing day-to-day operations. It was about creating a robust and unified culture where everyone understood the mission and worked together toward common goals. He realized that more was needed to assume that his senior management and team leaders would automatically understand and communicate this vision to their teams. Instead, he had to take full responsibility for ensuring that every employee, starting with the management team, was aligned with the company's direction. The success of the company, much like the success of a wolf pack, depended on this unity.

The Start of a Business Culture

Recognizing the need for change, Garth went to work. He knew that the company needed a guiding framework to keep everyone on the same page. To address this, he created a concise document to capture the message that every member of the company should understand and communicate. It was effectively a hymn sheet. This wasn't a document of rules and regulations, or the standard operating procedure (SOPs); it was a blueprint for the company's communication. It laid out the company's vision, mission, values, and core beliefs. Garth crafted these elements carefully, ensuring that they weren't just lofty ideals but actionable principles that could be applied across the business.

The vision he set forth was clear: to become the leading financial services firm in their region, offering personalized, reliable solutions to clients while maintaining ethical and sustainable business practices. The mission outlined how the company would achieve this by empowering both employees and clients with the tools and knowledge they needed to succeed. The values and beliefs emphasized teamwork, integrity, innovation, and respect—qualities that Garth believed were essential for both business success and a positive corporate culture.

Once the hymn sheet was created, Garth knew the actual work was just beginning. He trusted his senior management team and believed they were competent leaders, but he also knew that trust alone wasn't enough to ensure full alignment. It was his responsibility to make sure that this document became the foundation of the company's culture and that every team leader, down to the most junior employees, understood its significance. Garth realized that for this vision to become reality, he had to ensure that everyone not only followed the document but genuinely believed in it.

A New Leadership Style

Garth's leadership style evolved with this realization. He began holding regular meetings with his management team to discuss the company's direction and ensure that they were on the same page. These meetings weren't just about performance reviews or quarterly goals. They became opportunities to revisit the vision, assess how well it was being implemented, and discuss any areas where the team might be falling out of alignment. Garth also started visiting different departments to talk directly with employees. He wanted to hear their thoughts and make sure they felt connected to the company's mission.

As he continued to communicate the vision, Garth focused on building a culture where respect, not authority, guided leadership. He understood that if his leadership were based solely on his title as CEO, it would be difficult to inspire loyalty and collaboration. Instead, he sought to lead by example, showing that he valued his employees' input and trusted them to make decisions in line with the company's values. By empowering his immediate team and trusting them to pass on this empowerment to junior leaders, he was not just managing a company—he was cultivating future leaders.

This shift in leadership style had a profound impact on the company. The management team became more engaged, and team leaders took ownership of their roles, ensuring their teams were aligned with the company's direction. Employees at all levels started to see themselves as vital contributors to the company's success. The company hymn sheet became more than just a document; it became a living guide that shaped the way the business operated daily.

As a result, teamwork within the company improved significantly. Employees began to appreciate their unique roles within the organization, understanding how their contributions affected the larger goals. Like a well-coordinated wolf pack, the company now worked in harmony. Garth no longer worried that his management team was out of sync with his vision. Instead, he saw a group of leaders who were fully aligned with the company's goals and who were committed to leading their teams in the same direction.

By fostering a healthy corporate culture and focusing on clear communication, Garth became a leader who inspired respect, not because of his position but because of his actions.

Appendix B: Resources offers a basic, 10-point hymn sheet template for small businesses. It is in Word format, includes guiding notes and an example, and is editable for your requirements.

Case Study: A Strong Family with Collective Leadership

Ainsley and Tracy were recently married, both entering their second marriage with a deep commitment to making it work this time around. They each brought with them lessons from their past relationships, and both were determined to avoid the mistakes that had led to their previous divorces. Ainsley had no children of his own, while Tracy had two daughters, ages 8 and 12, who now lived with them full-time. It was a loving home, and Tracy's daughters accepted Ainsley as a father figure. However, the couple knew that keeping this balance required careful thought and conscious effort. They were resolute in their goal of building a healthy relationship and a strong family unit—a pack, as they often called it.

Their journey toward creating this strong family began with open communication. Before they officially blended their lives, Ainsley and Tracy spent hours discussing their roles within the family. They wanted to make sure they were fully coordinated, ensuring that their partnership was one of equals. Both were determined not to let past insecurities or miscommunication affect their new marriage. They realized that a strong partnership would serve as the foundation for a healthy family.

More importantly, they talked extensively about the family dynamics and how they would treat Tracy's daughters. For Ainsley, this was particularly significant because he didn't want the girls to feel like stepchildren. He insisted they would be treated as if they were his own. Tracy agreed, knowing that this level of commitment from Ainsley was vital for the emotional security of her daughters. They both knew that treating the children equally was crucial for fostering a sense of unity in their home. This shared decision showed their collective leadership wisdom, ensuring that no one felt isolated or left out.

A Set of Values

They didn't stop at just discussing roles, though. Ainsley and Tracy knew that words had to be backed by action. Together, they developed a set of family values that would guide their daily lives. They wanted these values to be clear, simple, and relatable, even for their youngest daughter, who was only eight years old. The couple wanted to create a solid foundation for their family based on principles everyone could understand and follow, regardless of age.

After much thought, they came up with four overarching values that they believed would help them lead by example rather than exerting parental dominance. These values were honesty, kindness, neatness, and friendliness. Ainsley and Tracy felt these were not just words but guiding principles that would encourage mutual respect and foster a positive environment.

They carefully explained each value to the girls, making sure the meanings were clear:

- Honesty: We are always honest in what we say or do.

- Kindness: We are always kind to others—people and animals.

- Neatness: We always clean up after we've messed up.

- Friendliness: We always greet everybody when we arrive or depart.

To reinforce these values, they decided to make them a visible part of their home. They printed out the values in large, colorful letters and placed them on the refrigerator door, held in place by magnets. The girls were excited to help, adding their own drawings and decorations to the display. By placing the values in such a central location, Ainsley and Tracy ensured that the whole family would be constantly reminded of them. It wasn't just about telling the children what to do; it was about showing them how to live by these principles every day.

The couple also made a point of referring to the values regularly. Whenever someone stepped out of line, instead of simply scolding or speaking down to the child, they reminded them of the family values. For example, if one of the girls didn't clean up after herself, Tracy might say, "Remember, neatness is one of our values. Let's make sure we clean up." In doing this, they avoided harsh punishments or long lectures, focusing instead on reinforcing the behavior they wanted to see. And when someone displayed positive behavior, they made sure to acknowledge it. "I noticed you were kind to your sister today. Thank you," Ainsley would say, making sure the girls knew their efforts were appreciated.

Mutual Support and Trust

This approach began to pay off. The girls, like all children, still went through their difficult moments, particularly during their teenage years. There were arguments and challenges, as there are in any family, but the difference was the foundation of trust and open communication that Ainsley and Tracy had built. Problems were discussed openly, and everyone understood that they had a role in supporting one another. The girls felt safe coming to Ainsley and Tracy with their concerns, knowing they would be met with understanding and guidance rather than judgment.

As the years passed, the strength of this family unit only grew. The girls began to embrace their roles, not only within the family but also in their friendships and school life. The values that Ainsley and Tracy had instilled into them became second nature. Even when faced with challenges outside the home, they carried these lessons with them, whether it was showing kindness to a struggling friend or staying honest in tricky situations.

In the end, Ainsley and Tracy's decision to lead their family through collective leadership rather than dominance had a profound effect. They had built a home based on mutual respect, open communication, and shared values. The result was a strong family bond that allowed each member to feel valued and supported. Their little bit of family leadership truly went a long way.

Appendix B: Resources offers a one-page example of how family values can be displayed. It is in Word format and needs your creative touch to add color, pictures, or photos.

Reflection

The stories of Thorne, Garth, and Ainsley offer a wealth of insight into leadership, teamwork, and family dynamics, illustrating how important it is to be intentional in our roles in business and personal life.

Whether we are leading a company or nurturing a family, these examples show that leadership isn't about force or authority but about guiding others with purpose, understanding, and respect. The lessons learned from the wolf pack and the subsequent case studies can be applied to many aspects of life, allowing us to reflect on our current practices and consider areas where we can grow as leaders.

In the business world, Garth's journey highlights the importance of clear communication and shared values. It's not enough for a CEO to simply issue orders and expect employees to follow. Authentic leadership involves creating an environment where everyone understands the vision and feels like an essential part of the company's success. When Garth took the time to realign his management team and ensure that everyone from the top down understood the company's goals, he saw a significant improvement in teamwork and morale. This shift didn't happen because of Garth's position as CEO but because of the respect he earned by leading through example and fostering a sense of belonging.

The same principles apply to family life. Ainsley and Tracy's story proves how intentional leadership can help create a supportive and cohesive family unit. By establishing shared values and leading with consistency, they built a home where respect and trust were the cornerstones. Like the wolves that support each other in their pack, families thrive when every member understands their role and works together toward a common goal. Leadership in family life, just like in business, is about creating a space where everyone feels heard and valued.

Reflecting on these examples, it's important to ask yourself how you currently approach leadership and team dynamics, both at work and at home. Do you lead with authority, or do you foster a culture of collaboration and respect? Are the people in your team—or your family—clear on their roles and contributions, or is there confusion and misalignment? As you consider your leadership style, think about how well you communicate your vision. Do you ensure that everyone understands the shared goals, or do you assume they will figure it out on their own?

At work, it may be helpful to reflect on how aligned your team is with the company's mission and values. Are there clear principles that guide daily decision-making? And more importantly, are you, as a leader, embodying those principles? Garth's case reminds us that leadership is about more than setting expectations; it's about living the values you want to see reflected in your team. How are you modeling the behavior you expect from others? Are you providing opportunities for others to lead and grow, or are you holding on to control?

In your personal life, consider how well your family is functioning as a unit. Do you and your partner discuss roles and responsibilities openly, as Ainsley and Tracy did, or is there a need for clarity in who takes on what? Are the values of your household clear to everyone, especially your children? Leadership in the home, much like in the workplace, is not about dominance but about guiding and supporting each other. Think about how you manage conflict in your family—do you reinforce positive behavior, or is most of your energy spent reacting to problems? Ainsley and Tracy's example reminds us that consistency and positive reinforcement can go a long way in building strong, resilient relationships.

These reflective questions can help you identify areas where you may want to make changes, but they also serve as a reminder that leadership is a dynamic process. There's no perfect formula, and the journey of self-improvement is ongoing. The key takeaway is that whether you're leading in a corporate environment or guiding your family, the principles of respect and shared values are universal. As you continue to reflect on your leadership style, ask yourself how you can better support those around you, foster collaboration, and build a stronger sense of unity—whether in your team or your home.

Action Plan

Business Culture with a Hymn Sheet

Create a concise hymn sheet outlining your company's vision, mission, values, and beliefs. Make sure these principles are clear, actionable, and relatable to all employees. Distribute the document and hold regular discussions with your team to ensure alignment. Lead by example by embodying these values in your daily decisions and interactions. Reinforce the culture by recognizing employees who model the company's values and consistently refer to the hymn sheet when addressing issues or making strategic decisions.

Family Culture with Guiding Values

Develop a set of guiding values for your family. These should be simple and easy to understand for all family members, regardless of age. Post these values in a visible place and explain their importance. Lead by example by living these values every day, ensuring that your actions align with the principles you've set. When conflicts arise, remind family members of shared values, and reinforce positive behaviors by acknowledging them.

Chapter 2
Adaptability, Resilience, and Resourcefulness

"In the wild, survival depends on cooperation, on the strength of the pack" - Farley Mowat

Thorne's First Winter

As the vibrant hues of summer began to fade, Thorne sensed an unfamiliar shift in the world around him. The air, once filled with the warmth of the sun, now carried a crispness that hinted at the challenges ahead. The leaves in the forest, once green and full of life, began to turn golden and brittle, signaling the arrival of fall. For Thorne, this was the first time he would experience the change of seasons, and he had much to learn.

Thorne was no longer the tiny pup that nestled against his mother, surviving solely on her nourishing milk. At five months old, he was weaning—transitioning from a diet of milk to the tougher sustenance of solids. This shift, while gradual, marked a crucial step in his development. It was not just about nourishment but a lesson in adaptability. He was learning to live like a loyal member of the pack, relying on the same resources that sustained the adults.

Adaptability

In the days leading up to winter, the pack seemed to grow more restless. The abundance of summer prey was dwindling, and each hunt became more vital than the last. Thorne watched as the older wolves, once leisurely in their movements, became more focused. Every action was deliberate—whether it was hunting, guarding the den, or simply grooming one another. There was a tension in the air, a quiet understanding that the easy days of summer were behind them, and the most challenging season was about to begin.

The first snowfall came suddenly, transforming the forest into a world of white. At first, Thorne was fascinated by the soft blanket that covered the ground. The snow muted the usual sounds of the forest, creating a sense of stillness. But with the snow came biting winds that stung his nose and chilled his small frame. He quickly realized that winter was not just a time of beauty—it was a test of endurance.

The pack was on the move constantly, driven by the need to find food. Thorne, still weaning, struggled to keep up. His body was not yet used to the solid food he was beginning to eat, and his energy waned faster than the adults. As they moved through the snow-covered forest, he felt the cold sap his strength. Each step became more difficult as his paws sank into the soft, wet snow. The once playful bounds of his youth were replaced by measured, careful movements.

Despite these challenges, Thorne observed the adaptability of the pack. The wolves, though burdened by the harsh conditions, found ways to adjust. Hunting was different now. The snow, though an obstacle for Thorne, provided the pack with a unique advantage. Their thick fur insulated them against the cold, and their long legs allowed them to move through the deep snow with ease. Smaller predators struggled in these conditions, giving the wolves a competitive edge. Thorne watched as the older wolves taught the younger ones how to conserve energy by moving strategically through the drifts, using the terrain to their advantage.

Resilience

But even with these adaptations, food was becoming scarce. Some days, the pack returned empty-handed; their energy was spent with nothing to show for it. Thorne experienced hunger for the first time in his life—an empty ache that gnawed at him as the days without food stretched on. His body, still developing, was vulnerable to these shortages. He had never gone so long without nourishment, and the feeling of hunger was as sharp as the frigid wind that whipped through the trees. Yet, this was his first lesson in resilience.

Thorne learned to endure the hunger, just as the rest of the pack did. His mother, though no longer able to provide him with all the milk he needed, still shared what little she could. But even this was not enough. Thorne had to rely more on his strength, slowly learning to survive on the scraps that the pack scavenged. In the depths of winter, scavenging became a necessity. The wolves turned to carrion, feeding on the remains of animals that had succumbed to the cold. It was not the fresh, warm meat of a successful hunt, but it was enough to keep them going. Thorne's diet shifted, and he had no choice but to adapt.

As the days passed, Thorne noticed the pack's reduced activity. During the colder months, they conserve energy by staying close to the den, moving only when necessary. The constant roaming of summer gave way to a more strategic existence. They moved with purpose—whether it was for hunting or seeking shelter from the worst of the storms. Thorne also noticed how the wolves groomed each other more often during these times. Grooming was not just about cleanliness; it was a way to strengthen social bonds, a reminder that even in the harshest conditions, they were still a pack.

The cold, relentless and unforgiving, took its toll on all of them. But through the difficult days, Thorne learned a critical lesson—resilience is about more than physical endurance. It is about the mental strength to keep going, even when everything feels stacked against you. As the weeks wore on, Thorne watched how the pack worked together to survive. They shared what little food they had, took turns keeping watch, and huddled together for warmth on the coldest nights. The pack's unity was their greatest strength, and Thorne was slowly beginning to understand his place within it.

Resourcefulness

There were days when Thorne doubted his ability to survive the winter. The hunger, the cold, and the endless struggle to keep up with the adults weighed heavily on him. But each challenge forced him to grow stronger. He learned to pace himself, to rely on the older wolves for guidance, and to find strength in the bonds that tied the pack together.

As the snow piled deeper and the nights grew longer, Thorne began to see that winter, though harsh, had its rhythm. The pack's survival depended not just on brute strength or speed but on its ability to adapt to the ever-changing environment. They were forced to become scavengers, move with the storms instead of against them, and rely on each other in ways that were not necessary in the abundant days of summer.

Thorne's first winter was a trial by fire—an initiation into the realities of life as a wolf. He was no longer the carefree pup of summer. He had been tested by the cold and the scarcity of food, and in the process, he had learned invaluable lessons in adaptability and resilience. The winter was not over, but Thorne had already grown in ways he could not have imagined when the first snowflakes began to fall.

Real – Life Example: Manufacturing Resilience in Tough Times

Businesses, like wolf packs, often experience their own "winters"—times when the environment shifts and survival becomes a daily struggle. The key to thriving through these challenging times is adaptability and resilience, just as wolves must adapt to a changing landscape. This case study illustrates the story of a manufacturing company that faced its own "winter" but found ways to endure and ultimately emerge stronger.

Case Study: IronPro Manufacturing's Winter

IronPro Manufacturing was a thriving mid-sized company specializing in steel props used for roof supports in mining operations. For years, it was a leader in its industry, supplying props to major mining companies worldwide. Its reputation for quality and reliability kept its order books full, and business was booming. However, a worldwide economic downturn coupled with a decline in mining operations caused a sharp drop in demand for its steel props.

The global mining industry was suffering. Commodity prices were falling, forcing mining companies to cut back on production. Many mines also began seeking cheaper alternatives to traditional steel props to lower their operational costs. IronPro Manufacturing quickly realized that without significant adaptation, it would not survive this slump.

The Shift to Roof Bolts

Facing plummeting demand for steel props, IronPro began researching alternatives. Roof bolts, already used in some mining operations, offered a more cost-effective and efficient solution. They could be installed more quickly, needed less material, and allowed for better long-term structural stability, making them an attractive alternative for cash-strapped mining companies.

However, developing roof bolts took time. The company needed to design a new product, test it extensively, and gain approval from mine engineers before they could begin full-scale production. While IronPro was confident that roof bolts would provide a lifeline, the process from development to approval could have been faster. In the meantime, the company had to find a way to survive.

Resilience Through Tough Measures

During this period of uncertainty, IronPro Manufacturing implemented five key measures to keep the business afloat, though many were tough decisions:

Cost Cutting: The company had to reduce operational expenses significantly. This included cutting non-essential staff and scaling back on administrative costs. Although layoffs were painful, they were necessary to keep the core team employed and operational.

Wage Reductions: To avoid deeper cuts, IronPro's leadership made the difficult decision to temporarily reduce wages. Employees were asked to take a 15% pay cut, with the understanding that wages would be restored once the company recovered. This shared sacrifice helped to keep the company solvent.

Negotiating Supplier Contracts: IronPro renegotiated its contracts with suppliers, seeking discounts or extended payment terms. By carefully managing its cash flow, the company was able to continue sourcing raw materials, even as revenue declined.

Leaning on Reserves: The company used its cash reserves to bridge the gap between reduced sales and ongoing expenses. While this was a risky move, depleting reserves during a downturn, it allowed IronPro to stay operational and continue product development.

Deferred Maintenance: Routine maintenance on non-essential equipment was postponed. Although this presented some risks, prioritizing essential operations over minor maintenance ensured that production could continue without significant interruptions.

While these strategies helped the company survive, they also damaged morale and operations. IronPro was still far from being out of the woods, and further action was needed to stay viable.

Exploring New Markets

Realizing that waiting for the mining industry to recover could take years, IronPro turned to non-mining markets to generate cash flow. The company began manufacturing products they had never considered before. This strategy, while unconventional, proved to be a lifeline.

Agricultural Equipment Parts: IronPro used its metalworking expertise to produce parts for tractors and other farm machinery. This unexpected market helped the company generate revenue during the off-season for mining.

Custom Steel Furniture: IronPro found a niche in high-end, custom-made steel furniture for commercial spaces. While less lucrative than their primary business, this venture allowed them to keep their workforce employed and maintain cash flow.

Structural Supports for Construction: The company also supplied steel supports for construction companies working on infrastructure projects. These supports, while smaller in scale than those used in mining, provided a new market that helped fill the gap left by declining mining demand.

While not aligned with IronPro's core business, these ventures kept the company alive during the leanest months. They allowed IronPro to continue paying its employees, keep its skilled workforce, and maintain cash flow, even as its mining revenues remained low.

Emerging Stronger

After months of development and testing, IronPro's roof bolts were finally ready for the market. The company secured several contracts with mining firms that were eager to reduce their costs while maintaining safety standards. The new product line allowed IronPro to return to profitability, albeit at a slower pace than before the downturn.

IronPro Manufacturing's story is about resilience and adaptability. Like a wolf pack facing the challenges of winter, the company had to adjust its strategies to survive. By diversifying its product offerings, cutting costs, and keeping a commitment to its workforce, IronPro not only weathered the storm but emerged stronger. The development of roof bolts was the key to their long-term recovery, but it was the company's adaptability during the lean times that indeed ensured their survival.

Real – Life Example: Finding Strength in the Unexpected

Life is full of unexpected turns, and like businesses that must adapt in challenging times, we as individuals often discover our resilience when facing our own "winters." Adaptability, although usually difficult, allows us to survive and eventually thrive when life doesn't go as planned. This is the story of Sarah, a young woman who, through immense personal tragedy and hardship, found the strength to persevere.

A Mother's Strength: Navigating Life's Unplanned Journey

Sarah had always been career-focused. As a rising marketing professional at a mid-sized firm, she had built a solid foundation for her future. She and her husband, Marcus, were not planning to have children anytime soon. But when she discovered she was pregnant, the initial shock quickly gave way to excitement. While the pregnancy was unplanned, they saw it as an unexpected blessing. As the news settled in, they began to prepare. Their finances were stable, and although there were concerns, they felt confident they could make it work.

However, just as they started to see a clear path ahead, tragedy struck. Marcus died suddenly in a car accident, leaving Sarah devastated and reeling. In an instant, the future they had envisioned together vanished. The overwhelming grief and pain seemed impossible to bear. She was pregnant, alone, and her world had turned upside down.

The days following Marcus's death were a blur of sadness, disbelief, and despair. Sarah was left not only to grapple with her grief but also with the weight of her new reality—raising a child without her partner. The uncertainty about how she would manage financially and emotionally loomed large. Every day felt like a battle between sinking into the deep sorrow she felt and forcing herself to think about the baby's future. It was in this space, between love and loss, that Sarah had to find her resilience.

Her employer played a pivotal role in helping her during this time. Recognizing her emotional and physical exhaustion, they extended her maternity leave with added time off to recover after the birth. While the leave came with a reduced salary, it was an act of deep empathy. It gave Sarah the space she needed to grieve and prepare for her new life as a single mother. Her employer's understanding and flexibility were lifelines during those first painful months.

The birth of her son changed everything. Holding him for the first time, Sarah felt an overwhelming sense of responsibility. He needed her, and it awakened a strength she didn't know she possessed. The thought of his survival became her central focus. There were sleepless nights, moments of intense loneliness, and the constant longing for Marcus to share these moments. But as difficult as it was, baby Jack became the anchor that kept her grounded. She realized that her resilience wasn't just about her survival—it was about his, too.

Sarah's family, particularly her sister and mother, stepped in to support her. They helped by caring for Jack and providing her with emotional and practical support. Their presence was a source of comfort, allowing Sarah to catch her breath when the weight of her new reality felt too heavy to bear. With their help, she started to regain her footing. She began to understand that while life had forced her into a tricky situation, she had the strength to endure it.

During her extended leave, Sarah had the time and space to think about the future. She knew she couldn't return to her previous role in the same capacity—full-time work in the office was no longer an option. She needed to be at home for Jack, but she also needed to maintain some form of income. After much reflection, she approached her employer with a plan. She proposed taking on a lesser role that allowed her to work remotely. Her employer, recognizing her talents and value, agreed. This new arrangement gave Sarah the flexibility she needed while still contributing to the company.

With a reduced but steady income, Sarah began exploring other ways to generate revenue from home. She realized that her marketing and communications skills could be used for freelance work, which she could do in her own time, at her own pace. Slowly but surely, she built up a portfolio of clients, supplementing her income and giving her a sense of control over her financial situation.

As the months passed, Sarah found a rhythm. She settled into a routine that worked for both her and Jack. It wasn't easy, and there were still moments of profound grief, but she had created a stable life, even if it wasn't the one she had imagined. Jack was thriving, and while Sarah was not financially flush, she was secure. She had made it through the worst of the storm, finding strength she hadn't known existed.

Sarah's story is one of resilience, adaptability, and the power of love. Like businesses that must pivot to survive harsh conditions, Sarah had to find new ways to navigate her life in the absence of her partner. It wasn't a path she would have chosen, but it was one she learned to walk with grace and strength. Her ability to adapt to her new circumstances, with the support of her family and employer, allowed her to create a life where she could be both present for her son and financially stable.

Sarah's experience reminds us all that even when life throws us into our darkest winters, there is still hope. With resilience and adaptability, we can find our way through, even when the road is hard.

Insights

Adaptability and resilience are critical qualities that help individuals and businesses navigate uncertain times. These traits are not just survival mechanisms but are essential for growth and progress. The following five quotes from prominent thinkers illuminate these principles and demonstrate how they can be applied both in personal life and the world of business.

Charles Darwin: "It is not the strongest of the species that survive, nor the most intelligent, but the one most responsive to change"

Darwin's observation emphasizes a crucial truth: the ability to adapt is far more important than strength or intelligence when faced with challenges. In the natural world, species survive not because they are the most powerful but because they learn to adjust to changing conditions. This principle holds true in business and life. For instance, a company might have the most advanced technology or the best resources, but if it does not respond to market shifts, it will not thrive. The same can be said for individuals facing personal difficulties. The strongest among us are not those who avoid hardship but those who can evolve in response to it. When we embrace change rather than resist it, we find new ways to survive—and even prosper.

Tony Robbins: "The quality of your life is in direct proportion to the amount of uncertainty you can comfortably deal with"

This quote highlights the reality that resilience is often about how much discomfort and ambiguity we are willing to tolerate. Life is inherently uncertain, and the more we can adapt to this fact, the more successful and fulfilled we can be. Consider someone going through a sudden loss or upheaval, whether personal or professional. Uncertainty will always be present, but learning to accept it without becoming overwhelmed is critical to moving forward. When we stop trying to control every variable and become more comfortable with the unknown, we reduce anxiety and open ourselves to new possibilities. Actual growth happens when we stop seeing uncertainty as something to fear and instead view it as an opportunity to reinvent ourselves.

Sheryl Sandberg: "You are not born with a fixed amount of resilience. Like a muscle, you can build it up, draw on it when you need it"

Resilience is not a finite resource. Like any skill or strength, it is something that can be developed over time. This perspective reframes hardship as a training ground for growth. Every challenge, whether it's navigating a problematic career change or surviving personal loss, is an opportunity to build resilience. Much like how muscles are strengthened through repeated use, resilience grows with each new obstacle we face. Over time, we can draw on this strength whenever we need it, making us more capable of handling future adversities. This is a comforting realization—it means that no matter how difficult things may seem, we have the potential to become stronger through the experience.

Maya Angelou: "You may not control all the events that happen to you, but you can decide not to be reduced by them"

Angelou's words serve as a reminder that while we cannot dictate the events that come our way, we are entirely in charge of how we respond to them. This is an empowering concept, especially when faced with personal tragedy or professional setbacks. Loss, failure, and disappointment are part of life's journey, but they do not have to define who we are or how our story unfolds. The strength of the human spirit lies in its ability to rise above circumstances and remain undiminished. Choosing not to be reduced by adversity is a powerful act of resilience, and it gives us control over our narrative even when external events feel overwhelming.

Viktor Frankl: "When we are no longer able to change a situation, we are challenged to change ourselves"

Frankl's insight touches on the profound adaptability of the human spirit. Sometimes, no matter how hard we try, the external circumstances of our lives refuse to change. Whether it's a declining industry or an unchangeable personal loss, there are moments when pushing against the tide is futile. In these moments, the only possibility left is to change ourselves—our perspective, our approach, or our expectations. IronPro's shift from manufacturing steel props to developing roof bolts is an example of this. Rather than resisting market changes, they adapted their business model. This shift in focus allowed them not only to survive but to find new avenues of success. When we stop trying to control the external world and instead focus on our transformation, we unlock the ability to thrive in even the most challenging circumstances.

Reflection

As we close this chapter, it's essential to pause and reflect on the deeper themes we've explored—adaptability, resilience, and resourcefulness. These qualities are not just theoretical ideas but practical tools we all must use to navigate the inevitable challenges of life. Whether in business or personal circumstances, we are constantly presented with situations that test our ability to adjust, endure, and find new paths forward.

Take a moment to think about a recent challenge you've faced. It could be a disruption in your professional life, like a shift in market demand, a business downturn, or even a restructuring at work. Or perhaps it's something personal—maybe a sudden change in your health, a family loss, or an unexpected financial strain. How did you respond to this challenge? Did you find yourself adapting quickly, or were there moments when you felt overwhelmed by the uncertainty? Reflection gives us the chance to evaluate not just what we did but how we could have done better.

In business, adaptation often requires us to let go of old methods and embrace new ones. For a company like IronPro, the shift from manufacturing steel props to developing roof bolts wasn't an easy one. It required foresight, flexibility, and patience. But, most importantly, it required the willingness to pivot when the old way of doing things no longer worked. In your own professional life, there may be times when the strategies that once brought success no longer yield the same results. Have you been able to spot these moments? Did you resist change at first, or did you see it as an opportunity to innovate and grow?

Now, turn your attention to your personal life. Personal challenges often carry a more profound emotional weight, but they are no less navigable with the right mindset. When Sarah lost her husband unexpectedly, she faced a crossroads. The life she had envisioned disappeared in an instant. Yet, through that hardship, she found resilience—drawing strength from her son, her family, and her inner drive to keep going. Her experience teaches us that even when we are plunged into circumstances we never wanted or expected, there is always a way to move forward.

So, as you reflect on your journey, consider this: What have you learned about yourself in the face of hardship? Did you discover a hidden strength, or did you find new ways to cope with uncertainty? Resilience is often born in these moments when we least expect it, and while the process may be uncomfortable, it's through that discomfort that growth occurs.

Looking forward, how can you apply these lessons to future challenges? Whether it's pivoting your business strategy or finding new ways to balance personal commitments, your capacity to adapt and endure is your most valuable asset. The key is to remain open to change, even when it is painful. Remember, resilience is not something we are born with—it's something we develop over time with each new challenge, failure, or setback.

The goal is not to avoid hardship but to learn from it. When the next challenge comes—and it will—you'll be better prepared to meet it head-on. You'll know that even in the face of overwhelming odds, you can adapt, grow, and find a way through. The strength to do so is already within you; sometimes, it just takes a challenge to reveal it.

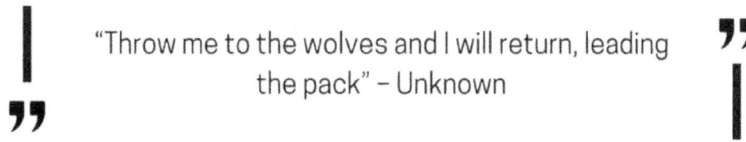

"Throw me to the wolves and I will return, leading the pack" – Unknown

Action Plan

Taking the lessons of adaptability and resilience into your daily life requires intentional action. Here is a simple, actionable plan you can implement.

Identify Challenges

Make a habit of regularly identifying both personal and professional challenges. Being aware of your challenges is the first step.

Evaluate Your Response

After identifying a challenge, reflect on how you typically respond. Do you resist change, or do you adapt? Be honest with yourself and think about how you could improve your response to future obstacles.

Develop Adaptability Skills

Train yourself to be more adaptable by actively seeking opportunities to embrace change. Start small—try a novel approach to an old task or embrace modern technology. Building adaptability in small ways will prepare you for bigger shifts.

Build Resilience

Focus on building resilience over time. This could involve improving your critical thinking skills, developing a more robust support network, or setting small, achievable goals that foster perseverance.

Reflect and Adjust

Set time aside every week to reflect on your progress. How have you adapted? What have you learned? Use this reflection to adjust your strategies and continually improve.

Chapter 3

Communication and Social Bonds

"A wolf's howl is a cry for companionship, a plea for acceptance, a hunger for belonging" - Unknown

Thorne's First Howl

Winter was loosening its icy grip on the land. The snow was no longer thick and endless but thinning, revealing patches of brown earth. For Thorne, now nearly a year old, this transition from winter to spring marked a new chapter in his life. He was no longer the fragile pup clinging to his mother. His legs were stronger, his body lean and agile, and though not yet fully grown, he could run alongside the pack.

Thorne was still learning the ways of the pack, but he had gained enough strength to follow them on their hunts. His role was still that of an observer, learning from the older wolves and testing his endurance with each chase. However, there was something more than physical growth that made this time significant. It was the time he would learn the true power of communication within the pack—his first howl was approaching.

As the winter gave way to the early signs of spring, the pack became more active. The sharp chill in the air began to ease, replaced by a softer breeze that carried the scents of new life. Small animals started to appear, and the promise of food lifted the spirits of the wolves. The once silent and snowy forest now echoed with the rustle of trees, the trickle of thawing streams, and the distant calls of birds returning from their winter migration. Thorne, feeling the changing energy, knew something new awaited him.

The pack gathered that evening under the pale glow of the moon. The air was clear, the night calm, and the time was right for a howl. Thorne had heard the pack howl many times before, but he had never joined them. Tonight, though, he would take his place among them. It wasn't a decision he made; it was a calling that he could no longer ignore.

The pack leader, a large, formidable wolf with fur that glistened silver in the moonlight, raised his head first. The deep, resonant howl that followed seemed to shake the very air around them. One by one, the other wolves joined in, each with their distinct voice. Thorne stood still for a moment, unsure. He had felt this moment coming, the pull to join his voice with theirs. But could he?

Then, instinct took over. Thorne raised his head, tilted his muzzle towards the sky, and let out his first tentative howl. It wasn't as strong or deep as the others, but it was his. It was raw and pure, carrying with it a mix of excitement, pride, and a bit of uncertainty. Yet, something magical happened as soon as the sound left his throat—it melded with the voices of the pack, becoming part of the larger whole.

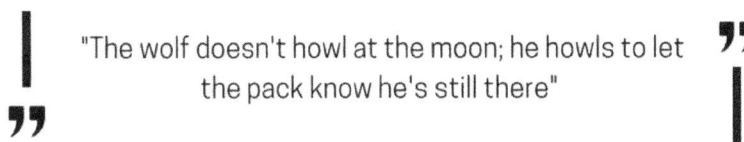

"The wolf doesn't howl at the moon; he howls to let the pack know he's still there"

Wolves have a unique way of communicating through their howls. Each wolf's howl is distinct, much like human fingerprints. Thorne's howl, though young and still developing, was already unique to him. As his voice joined the chorus, he could feel the power of their unity. The howling wasn't just noise; it was a way to bind them together, a social bond that transcended words. In that moment, Thorne felt truly part of the pack, as if his voice had been waiting all along to be heard.

The howling served many purposes, and Thorne was beginning to understand that. The wolves didn't just howl for the sake of it. Their howls could travel up to 16 kilometers in open terrain, allowing them to communicate over vast distances. If the pack were ever separated during a hunt or due to other circumstances, the howls would help them find one another again. Tonight, though, there was no urgency—this was a howl of celebration and unity, a reaffirmation of their bond as a pack.

As the howls echoed across the forest, it was clear that the wolves were also marking their territory. Their voices carried a message to any other packs that might be listening: this land was theirs. Howling was not just an act of communication; it was an assertion of strength and ownership. Thorne didn't fully grasp the depth of this yet, but he could sense the confidence in the pack's collective voice.

But there was something more personal in the howl, something Thorne felt deep in his chest as his voice mingled with the others. It was an emotional expression, a release. For Thorne, this first howl was more than a test of his voice—it was a statement that he belonged. The older wolves howled with a sense of pride, strength, and familiarity, while Thorne's howl was laced with the thrill of discovery.

The howling went on for what felt like hours, though it was likely just minutes. When the voices finally fell silent, the night seemed stiller than before. The bond within the pack felt more vigorous, and the silence that followed filled with an unspoken understanding. Thorne lowered his head and looked around at the others. The alpha wolf caught his gaze for a moment, and though no words were exchanged, Thorne felt acknowledged. His first howl was complete, and he had done it with his pack.

As the pack settled back into their routine, Thorne lay down near his mother. His body was still humming with the energy of the moment. He had howled with the pack, his voice joining the chorus of wolves who had come before him. It was a moment of unity, of communication, but more than anything, it was a moment of belonging.

Thorne's first howl had marked a new chapter in his life. He wasn't just following the pack now—he was a part of it. He had found his voice, and it would only grow stronger with time.

Real-Life Story: *The Bond of Words*

Liam and Emily knew from the start that their connection was special. They were sure they had found their soul mates in each other. But they also knew that love wasn't something that simply flourished on its own. It required care, attention, and effort. To them, a strong relationship was built on more than just shared experiences—it was rooted in deep communication and understanding.

From the beginning, they were committed to making their relationship meaningful. They decided to create a communication plan—a deliberate system designed to foster openness, trust, and emotional bonding. They didn't want to leave their relationship to chance. Together, they would ensure they stayed connected not just physically but emotionally and intellectually.

The system they developed was simple but effective. They called it their "Weekly Check-In." Once a week, they would set aside uninterrupted time to talk. It wasn't a rigid structure but a loose framework that allowed them to share their thoughts and feelings openly. They would each take turns speaking while the other listened without interruption. This ensured that they both felt heard and understood.

They divided their discussions into three categories: *dreams, fears, and love*. Dreams allowed them to share their hopes and aspirations. Whether it was about their careers, personal growth, or plans for the future, they could express their deepest desires without fear of judgment. By sharing these dreams, they felt more connected, as if they were building a future together piece by piece.

The next part of their system involved sharing their fears. They knew that vulnerability was key to a deep connection, so they made a point of talking about their worries—whether big or small. Fears about the relationship, personal insecurities, or external challenges were all discussed openly. This allowed them to confront issues before they could grow into larger problems, and it deepened their trust in each other.

Finally, they always ended their check-ins with expressions of love. This was their way of affirming the bond they shared. They talked about the things they appreciated in one another and what made them feel loved. These conversations didn't just maintain the emotional closeness—they reinforced it week after week.

Liam and Emily's communication system was a deliberate choice. It was not something that happened naturally but something they nurtured to deepen their relationship. The results were profound. Through consistent, meaningful conversations, they strengthened their emotional bond and gained a deeper understanding of each other.

Case Study: Strengthening the Pack Through Daily Communication

Garth had already made strides in improving communication within his company. He had successfully implemented the "hymn sheet" approach, ensuring that everyone in the organization was aligned with the company's core message and shared vision. His leadership had unified the team and created a sense of purpose. But despite this success, Garth sensed something was still missing.

The hymn sheet approach had helped with direction, but Garth noticed gaps in daily communication. While the company was moving in the right direction, employees were still relying on informal channels to stay updated on critical issues. This led to misunderstandings, rumors, and a lack of clarity at times. Garth, ever the problem solver, knew he had to find a way to close these communication gaps.

A Simple Solution

After reading extensively on business communication and discussing his concerns with peers, Garth found a potential solution. His research pointed to a need for more frequent, structured communication between team leaders and their teams. It wasn't enough to have the company aligned with a broader vision. There needed to be active, daily communication that connected every employee to the ongoing realities of the business.

Garth wasted no time. He called a meeting with his management team to discuss his findings. Using his natural communication skills, he laid out a plan to improve communication across the board. He explained how the new approach would not only prevent misunderstandings but also foster trust and cooperation within each team. The team leaders listened carefully, and thanks to Garth's transparent leadership style, they quickly bought into the idea.

Daily Structured Communication

The new system was simple yet effective. Garth instructed each team leader to spend 15 to 30 minutes with their teams every day. If they were not physically present, they could use conference calls to achieve the same goal. During these short, focused meetings, the team leader would update the group on key issues within the company. This approach eliminated speculation, prevented rumors, and allowed every employee to stay informed. Additionally, the team leader would share key priorities for their specific team, ensuring everyone understood what needed to be accomplished.

The most important aspect of these daily check-ins came at the end of the meeting. Garth encouraged the team leaders to ask each member if anything was preventing them from making progress on their tasks. This simple question opened the door for team members to share any obstacles or challenges they were facing. It also fostered an environment of support where team members could offer help or solutions to each other. Often, these offers came from unexpected or unlikely sources, further strengthening the bonds within the team.

Within a few months, the impact was evident. The company's communication had improved significantly. Rumors and misinformation were no longer a problem. Instead, employees felt informed and empowered. The daily check-ins became a vital part of the company's routine, not just to share information but to reinforce trust and transparency within teams.

The benefits didn't stop there. Garth noticed that the team leaders themselves had become more confident communicators and better leaders. By engaging in daily conversations with their teams, they developed more potent leadership skills. They learned how to listen effectively, address concerns, and offer guidance. This personal growth within the leadership ranks translated into a stronger company overall.

In the end, Garth's initiative had done more than just improve communication. It had built a stronger sense of unity within the company. Each team, much like a wolf pack, thrived on its ability to communicate clearly and support one another. The regular, structured communication ensured that everyone was working toward the same goals, with no one left behind.

Native Wisdom: Communication and Bonds Among People

Native American cultures have long understood the significance of communication and social bonds. For many nations, the lessons they observed from nature, including wolves, played a key role in shaping their approach to community and leadership. Among the Blackfoot, Cheyenne, Sioux, and Chinook nations, open communication and strong bonds among people were not only survival tools but also ways to maintain harmony and cohesion in their societies. Their wisdom passed down through stories, rituals, and sayings, continues to offer valuable insights into the power of communication in strengthening the bonds between individuals and communities.

The Circle of Communication: Blackfoot Wisdom

The Blackfoot people, who lived in the vast plains of North America, believed in the sacredness of the circle. For them, communication was a continuous flow where everyone had a voice, and the community thrived on the exchange of ideas, experiences, and emotions. The circle symbolizes unity, equality, and respect for all voices, regardless of rank or status.

One of the most important gatherings for the Blackfoot was the council circle, where leaders and elders would meet to discuss matters affecting them. The tradition was built on the idea that no one person held all the answers. Every individual had something valuable to contribute, and it was through listening that the best decisions could be made. The Blackfoot believed that, much like the wolves they shared the land with, their strength came from unity and mutual respect. Each voice in the circle was as essential as the next, reflecting the proverb, "The strength of the wolf is in the pack."

This practice of inclusive communication fostered trust and a sense of belonging within the community. It was understood that everyone's opinion mattered, creating an environment where people felt heard and valued. The Blackfoot's approach to communication serves as a reminder that listening is just as essential as speaking in building lasting bonds.

The Sacred Language of the Cheyenne

For the Cheyenne, language was sacred, and communication was an expression of the spirit. They believed that words carried power—both to heal and to harm. As a result, they were careful with their speech, teaching their children from an early age to use words with intention and respect. In Cheyenne culture, silence was also a form of communication, often more powerful than words. It was used to show deep respect, particularly in moments of reflection or mourning. It was also employed in other contexts, such as during a tense situation or when words might be inappropriate.

One Cheyenne story tells of a chief who, in his old age, called a meeting with his tribe. His body was weak, and his voice was soft, but his wisdom was vast. Instead of commanding the group with loud words, he spoke quietly, forcing the people to lean in and listen carefully. The silence that surrounded his words gave them weight and meaning. This chief's approach to communication mirrored the wolves' howls, which were not loud for volume's sake but were intentional, carrying meaning across great distances.

In this way, the Cheyenne valued the depth of communication. Their proverbs reflect this belief: *"Listen, or your tongue will keep you deaf."* Communication was more than just an exchange of information; it was a tool to build deeper connections and mutual understanding.

Sioux Teachings: The Power of Unity

The Sioux, also known as the Lakota, Dakota, and Nakota, were known for their strong community bonds, rooted in both communication and mutual support. For them, the concept of *mitákuye oyás'iŋ* ("we are all related") was at the heart of their culture. This belief emphasized the interconnectedness of all beings—humans, animals, and nature. Their communication was grounded in this principle, understanding that their words and actions had ripple effects that could strengthen or weaken the fabric of their community.

One Sioux ritual that embodied this was the Sun Dance. During the Sun Dance, the community came together in a powerful act of collective prayer and communication with the spirit world. This ceremony, which involved physical endurance, singing, and dancing, reinforced the bonds between the people and their connection to the earth and sky. It was through this shared experience that the Sioux people communicated their devotion to one another and the Great Spirit. The ritual also fostered a sense of unity and trust, essential for facing challenges both as individuals and as a community.

Their saying, "With all things and in all things, we are relatives," reminds us that the bonds we share with others, much like the bonds within a wolf pack, are vital for survival. Communication in Sioux culture was not just for practical purposes but was an act of acknowledging and reinforcing the web of relationships that sustained them.

Chinook Harmony: Communicating Across Waters

The Chinook people, who lived along the Columbia River, were expert traders and navigators. Their lives depended on their ability to communicate not only within their nation but with many others who traveled the rivers and coastlines of the Pacific Northwest. For the Chinook, communication was about keeping peace and fostering relationships with diverse groups of people. Their trading networks stretched for hundreds of miles, and their language, Chinook Jargon, became a tool for facilitating this communication across diverse cultures and languages.

The Chinook understood the value of clarity and respect in communication. Much like wolves who use their howls to identify themselves to their pack, the Chinook used language to build trust and ensure their survival. A saying from their elders reflects this: "When words become unclear, the heart follows." This saying speaks to the importance of clear communication, not just for practical exchanges but for supporting the trust and harmony that bound their communities together.

In their rituals and ceremonies, the Chinook placed great emphasis on singing and storytelling, which were ways of passing on knowledge and wisdom from generation to generation. These stories often reinforced the need for cooperation and understanding, highlighting that effective communication was the key to keeping peace within the community.

Modern Relevance

The wisdom of Native American cultures, particularly their emphasis on communication and social bonds, holds timeless value in our modern lives. In a world where technology often replaces face-to-face interaction, the principles of active listening, intentional speech, and mutual respect are more relevant than ever.

Whether in our families, workplaces, or communities, clear and purposeful communication fosters trust and strengthens relationships, much like it did for the Blackfoot, Cheyenne, Sioux, and Chinook. Their traditions remind us that every voice matters and that unity is built through shared understanding.

In our fast-paced world, taking the time to truly listen and engage with others—whether at home or in the office—can create bonds that are as strong and enduring as those in any tribe or wolf pack, encouraging harmony and collective growth in our daily lives.

Exploring Real Wolf Howls

This fascinating YouTube video presented by renowned wolf expert, Anneka Svenska, explores the various types of wolf howls and their meanings, much like how human communication shifts depending on context. From territorial howls to reunion calls, the video breaks down how wolves use their voices to express different emotions and communicate with their pack. By understanding these nuances, we can see how wolf communication mirrors the complexities of human speech across different situations.

 Click or scan this QR code to watch a video of wolf howls.

Reflection

As you reflect on this chapter, think about the ways communication has shaped your life. Whether in your relationships, at work, or in your community, communication is a fundamental part of how we connect with others. Like wolves, humans thrive when we understand how to express ourselves clearly and when we actively listen to those around us. This chapter explored the power of communication and the bonds it creates. Now, it's time to reflect on how you can apply these lessons in your own life.

Listening More Effectively

One of the most powerful aspects of wolf communication is their ability to listen. Their howls aren't just about being heard; they're also a way to connect with the pack, signaling their position, their intentions, and their emotions. Think about your listening habits. Do you truly listen when others speak, or are you simply waiting for your turn to talk? Active listening means being present and paying attention to both words and body language.

Speaking with Purpose

Wolves use their howls with intention. Every howl serves a specific purpose, whether it's to unite the pack, defend territory, or locate lost members. Similarly, the words we choose and how we say them carry weight. Are your words intentional, or do you sometimes speak without considering their impact? Clear and purposeful communication helps prevent misunderstandings and builds trust.

Building Stronger Bonds Through Communication

Like wolves, humans are social creatures who rely on strong bonds for survival and success. Healthy communication strengthens these bonds, whether in our personal relationships or professional environments. In this chapter, we've seen how daily check-ins in a business setting or weekly emotional check-ins in a relationship can create trust, prevent misunderstandings, and build unity.

Fostering an Environment of Trust

Trust is the foundation of any strong pack, and it's built through consistent and open communication. Wolves trust their pack members to protect them and work together for the good of all. In our lives, trust works the same way. When we communicate openly, we build trust, and when we trust others, we're more likely to feel supported and valued.

Adapting Your Communication Style

Just as wolves adjust their howls based on their needs, we, too, can adapt our communication styles depending on the situation. Communication with a partner may require more emotional openness, while business communication may need more clarity and structure. Understanding the context and adjusting accordingly is a key to effective communication.

Conclusion

This chapter explored the importance of communication through the lens of wolf behavior, Native wisdom, and practical examples. Now, it's your turn to apply these insights to your own life. Whether it's improving how you listen, speak, or build trust, the lessons here are a starting point for stronger, more meaningful connections in all areas of your life.

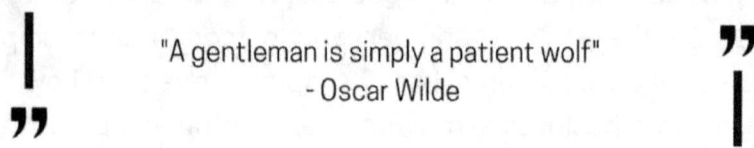

"A gentleman is simply a patient wolf"
- Oscar Wilde

Take time to reflect on how you can incorporate these practices into your daily routine. Remember, communication is not just about expressing yourself but also about creating a space where others feel heard and valued. As you strengthen your communication skills, you'll notice the positive ripple effects in your relationships, your work, and your community.

Action Plan

Here are suggestions for improving communication and social bonds.

Listening

The next time you're in a conversation, make a conscious effort to focus solely on what the other person is saying. Avoid interrupting, and instead, ask open-ended questions to show your interest. Try this for a week and reflect on how it changes your communication dynamic.

Speaking

Before you speak, especially in difficult conversations, pause to consider the outcome you hope to achieve. What message do you want to convey? Practicing this mindfulness before speaking can help ensure that your words align with your intentions.

Bonding

If you're part of a team, family, or social group, consider implementing regular check-ins. This could be a daily five-minute meeting at work to update everyone on key issues or a weekly one-on-one with a partner to discuss feelings, goals, and concerns. Regular, honest communication fosters a sense of belonging and keeps relationships strong.

Foster trust

To build trust, be transparent in your communication. If you're uncertain about something, express that uncertainty instead of pretending to have all the answers. Being honest, even when it's uncomfortable, creates a foundation of trust that strengthens every relationship.

Adapt

Reflect on the different people you communicate with daily. Are you adapting your communication style to suit each situation, or are you using the same approach in all settings? Try to adjust how you communicate depending on the needs and preferences of the person you're interacting with.

Chapter 4
Independence and Collaboration

"The wolf pack is a family. They hunt together, they
play together, and they protect each other" - Jack
London

Thorne's Path from Solitude to Strength

Thorne stood at the edge of the forest, his amber eyes
reflecting the soft light of the rising sun. The chill of the
morning air brushed against his fur, carrying with it the scent of
his pack. Behind him, the familiar sounds of the wolves waking
filled the air. His heart pounded, torn between the urge to stay

in the safety of the pack and the undeniable pull toward the unknown. He knew the time had come to leave. The alpha male, standing tall on a nearby ridge, watched in silence. There was no need for words. The alpha's gaze held both approval and understanding—Thorne was ready.

His legs felt heavy as he took his first steps away from the pack. Every instinct screamed to return to the comfort of the wolves he had grown up with, but a deeper force pushed him forward. Thorne had spent his youth learning the ways of the pack, but now, as a young adult, he had to find his path. His muscles tensed with the uncertainty of what lay ahead, yet there was excitement, too. He had to prove himself, to discover who he was beyond the protective structure of the pack.

Thorne moved swiftly through the trees, the sounds of the forest growing louder as he distanced himself from his family. The birds' songs were unfamiliar in this part of the woods, and the scent of prey lingered faintly on the breeze. His body instinctively lowered to the ground as he prepared to hunt alone for the first time. His stomach growled in protest—he had always relied on the pack for food, but now the responsibility rested solely on his shoulders.

Hours passed, and Thorne's first attempts at hunting ended in frustration. The deer were too fast, the rabbits too clever. His hunger deepened, but so did his resolve. He watched the animals carefully, learning their patterns and their weaknesses. Days later, he finally succeeded in bringing down a young hare. It wasn't much, but it was his first solo victory. The taste of the fresh kill filled him with a sense of independence he had never known before.

But independence came with its challenges. Thorne soon discovered that life outside the pack was harsher than he had imagined. The forest was vast, and danger lurked at every turn. He encountered other predators, and though he held his ground, the threat of injury was constant. The loneliness weighed on him, too. At night, as he curled up beneath the stars, he missed the warmth of his family, the sound of their howls in the distance.

After several weeks of solitude, Thorne's longing for the pack became too much to bear. He had learned much about surviving alone, but he felt incomplete. His heart ached for the bond he had shared with the wolves. One evening, as the sky darkened, he turned his nose toward the familiar scent of his pack and began the journey home.

When Thorne approached the den, the reaction was immediate. The wolves recognized him even before he reached the clearing. Their howls of excitement echoed through the trees, and Thorne's tail wagged uncontrollably in response. As he crossed the final distance, the wolves surrounded him, nipping playfully at his ears and jostling him with their bodies in a show of affection. The pack's acceptance was absolute, and Thorne realized at that moment just how much he had missed their presence.

The alpha male stood apart from the others, his eyes locked with Thorne's. There was pride in his gaze, not just for Thorne's return but for the lessons learned. Independence had been necessary, but now Thorne understood the deeper value of collaboration. The pack was not just a safety net—it was a source of strength, a system of support that allowed each wolf to thrive in ways they never could alone.

In the days that followed, Thorne reintegrated into the pack—his time away had changed him but for the better. He was more confident and more aware of his abilities. Yet, he also understood the limitations of solitude. Alone, he had been vulnerable. Together with the pack, he was nearly unstoppable. He watched as the wolves coordinated their hunts, moving as one fluid unit. Each member had a role to play, and through their collaboration, they achieved success far beyond what any solitary wolf could manage.

Thorne reflected on his journey. Independence had taught him self-reliance, but collaboration had shown him the power of unity. The strength of the pack did not lie in its numbers alone but in its ability to work together, to protect one another, and to share in both hardship and triumph. In this balance of independence and collaboration, Thorne had found his place, not just as a wolf within the pack but as a leader in his own right.

Wolf Wisdom for Business

"Do you think I should resign?" Nathan's voice was tense with anticipation as he looked across the table at his mentor. Greg, a retired business executive, had seen it all, and Nathan hoped his years of experience could help him make the right decision. Nathan had been wrestling with the idea of starting his own consulting business and wanted advice on whether it was the right time to leave his current job behind.

Greg leaned back in his chair, taking a moment before responding. His eyes, still sharp despite his years, revealed a man who had carefully considered these kinds of questions many times before. "The big question, huh? Should you stay, or should you go?" His tone was measured, without any rush to provide the answer. Greg knew all too well that these decisions couldn't be handed to someone; they had to be found within.

"I just keep thinking," Nathan continued, "I could grow more if I were on my own. I'd have more control over my time, choose my clients, and build something that's mine. I could set my own rules, write my own paycheck." His words came quickly, as though convincing himself as much as seeking Greg's guidance.

Greg's face softened into a knowing smile. "Independence is a tempting idea, no doubt. Being your own boss means making your own decisions, setting your own hours, and choosing the direction of your business. It sounds like real freedom." He paused for effect, watching Nathan carefully. "But it also means you shoulder all the responsibility. Have you really thought about what that entails?"

Nathan frowned slightly, leaning back. "I think so... I mean, I'm ready to work hard."

Greg nodded, acknowledging the young man's enthusiasm. "Work ethic is a big part of it, sure. But being on your own is about more than just working hard. Think of it like Thorne—the wolf from the story. When Thorne left the pack, he gained his independence, learned to hunt for himself, and made decisions alone. But with that freedom came real hardship. He didn't have the pack to support him. He was on his own, exposed to dangers and challenges he hadn't faced before."

Nathan shifted in his seat. "I know it would be tough, but I feel like I could handle it. I've learned a lot already, and I'm ready to grow."

Greg nodded again, but his tone grew more serious. "There's no doubt independence can teach you a lot—resilience, adaptability, and how to trust yourself. If you succeed, the rewards are yours. But let's not sugarcoat this. Independence also means you're alone when things go wrong. There's no safety net, no team to share the burden with when you're facing difficulties. You must be ready for that kind of isolation."

Nathan considered Greg's words, his earlier excitement tempered by the realities Greg had laid out. "But what if that's exactly what I need? To prove to myself that I can succeed on my own?"

Greg leaned forward, folding his hands on the table. "That's a valid reason. And I won't deny that there's immense value in learning to stand on your own two feet. But let's talk about the other side of the coin: collaboration. Thorne, after learning to survive on his own, returned to the pack. Why? Because even though he had become stronger, he realized that with the pack, he was far more capable than he ever could be alone. That's a lesson many people don't understand until it's too late."

"A wolf's wisdom is learned through the trials of survival"

Nathan raised an eyebrow, intrigued. "Collaboration?"

"Yes," Greg replied. "In business, as in nature, there is a strength that comes from working with others that you simply cannot replicate alone. Sure, being independent means you call the shots. But with a strong team or a network of collaborators, you're able to leverage talents and resources that are beyond your abilities. You'll face fewer risks, and you'll have support when you need it. It's not about giving up freedom; it's about amplifying your potential."

Nathan was listening intently now, his earlier confidence replaced with curiosity. "So, you're saying that staying in my current role could still help me grow?"

"Absolutely," Greg said, his tone more encouraging. "In an organization, you're surrounded by colleagues who bring different skills and perspectives to the table. You don't have to go it alone to grow. Learning to collaborate effectively—whether that's within a company or as an entrepreneur working with clients and partners—teaches you how to balance independence with the strength of a collective."

Nathan looked down for a moment, processing the new perspective. "But if I stay in my current role, won't I always be limited by what the organization wants me to do?"

Greg shook his head. "That's a common misconception. The truth is that great leaders within organizations often have more freedom than independent consultants. They know how to navigate the system, how to influence others, and how to create change from within. And when they need support, they have an entire team at their disposal."

Nathan sighed, his thoughts in a jumble. "It sounds like both paths have their pros and cons."

Greg smiled, knowing that Nathan was on the right track. "Exactly. There's no perfect answer, Nathan. Independence gives you control, but it comes with risks and isolation. Collaboration gives you access to more resources and support, but you need to learn how to navigate those relationships. Thorne learned to balance the two—so can you."

Nathan sat quietly for a while, then finally said, "I guess I need to figure out which matters more to me right now."

Greg nodded. "That's the crux of it. Ask yourself this: Are you seeking independence because you're genuinely ready for the challenges or because you're frustrated with your current role? And if you do go solo, how will you ensure you're not completely isolated? Can you still find ways to collaborate with others?"

Nathan's eyes widened. "So even if I go independent, I still need collaboration?"

"Absolutely," Greg said firmly. "No one succeeds entirely on their own. Whether you stay in your job or start your own business, the key to success is in balancing independence with strategic collaboration. Build strong relationships, lean on others when you need to, and always remember that there's strength in numbers—even for a lone wolf."

Nathan nodded slowly, feeling both challenged and inspired. "You've given me a lot to think about."

Greg smiled. "That's the idea. Take your time with this decision. Whatever you choose, just remember—no one reaches their full potential alone."

Wolf Wisdom for Our Lives

The Dance of Strength and Togetherness

There is a pull, a quiet beckoning toward solitude.
To stand alone, firm in the knowledge of self,
untouched by the hands of others.
It feels pure, this independence—a freedom untethered,
a path walked by a single set of footprints,
leaving no one to obscure the view ahead.

You are the architect, the builder of your world,
crafting each moment as you wish,
unrushed by another's needs,
unfettered by the weight of shared burdens.

There is power in this space, in this solitude.
You breathe deeper, step lighter,
the sky stretches endlessly above you,
and the horizon is yours to chase.
But in the quiet moments between steps,
there is a whisper.

It speaks of the other, the many, the shared.
It reminds you that while a single tree may stand tall,
a forest is stronger for its roots are intertwined.

To walk alone is to feel the weight of your own shadow,
but to walk together is to share the light.
The burdens we carry, though personal,
are lighter when shouldered by more than one.
There is no shame in leaning,
no weakness in holding out your hand.

The air grows colder when no one walks beside you.
The path, once straight, becomes winding,
and though you may be strong in body,
the spirit wearies without the warmth of others.

Collaboration is not the sacrifice of self,
but the elevation of the whole.
It is the harmony in the music,
where each note played alone is clear,
but together they form a symphony,
rich and full, a sound that carries farther
than any single note could hope to travel.

There is beauty in standing apart,
but there is power in coming together.
The lone wolf survives,
but the pack thrives.
And is it not in the thriving that we find our strength?
In the intertwining of our efforts,
the blending of our voices,
each one distinct, yet contributing to the whole.

To stand alone is to test your mettle,
but to stand with others is to forge it stronger.

A single flame burns bright,
but a fire made from many sparks lights the way.
And so we ask,
why choose one over the other,
when the path is meant for both?

We learn in solitude,
but we grow in community.
Independence teaches us to trust our steps,
but collaboration teaches us to reach beyond ourselves.

The greatest mountains are not climbed alone,
nor are they conquered in a crowd.
It is the balance of both—
the moments of isolation that sharpen the mind,
and the moments of unity that build the strength to rise higher.

In your life, there will be times to stand apart,
to carve your own path,
to feel the freedom of independence.
But never forget the power of togetherness,
the strength that comes from leaning on others
when the road is long and the sky is dark.

This is the dance we all must learn,
the rhythm of solitude and community,
where one does not diminish the other,
but instead enriches it.
For in the end, we are both—
the lone wolf and the pack.
The solitary flame and the roaring fire.
The single voice and the symphony.

And in this dance, we find our truth,
that independence and collaboration are not opposites,

but partners in the journey of life.
Each step forward is ours alone,
but the ground we walk on is shared.
The wind in our face is ours to feel,
but the warmth of the sun belongs to all.

We are never truly alone,
nor are we ever completely entwined.
We exist in the space between—
strong in ourselves, stronger together.
And it is here, in this balance,
that we discover our greatest strength.

Reflection

As you reach the end of this chapter, take a moment to reflect on the lessons you've explored. The tension between independence and collaboration is not a challenge you face alone—it's a universal truth that echoes through every aspect of life. In business, in relationships, and even in personal growth, finding balance is a journey we all undertake.

Think back to the moments when you stood alone, relying solely on your strength and judgment. What did you learn in those times? How did independence serve you, and where did it leave you wanting more? There is pride in self-reliance, but even the strongest among us can benefit from the shared strength of others.

Now, consider the times when collaboration lifted you. Who stood by your side? How did their presence, wisdom, or support help you achieve what you could not have done alone? Collaboration is not about surrendering control; it's about amplifying your potential through shared effort.

As you consider these questions, remember that you are not choosing between independence and collaboration. You are crafting a life that weaves both into a strong fabric. There will be times to stand apart, testing your mettle, and there will be times to lean on the support of others. Embrace both with confidence, knowing that each path brings its own value.

Action Plan

Here are suggestions for finding your balance between independence and collaboration.

Assess Your Current Situation

Identify whether you're currently leaning more towards independence or collaboration in your personal and professional life. Write down two situations where you acted independently and two where you collaborated with others. Reflect on the outcomes of each.

Define Your Goals

Decide on an area where you want to grow—whether it's improving your self-reliance or fostering better teamwork. Create a short-term goal that emphasizes the area you need to develop. For example, if you want to strengthen your independence, set a goal to take on a solo project. If you want to work on collaboration, seek out a partnership or group project.

Find Your Balance

Commit to blending independence and collaboration. Identify one task or challenge on which you can work independently, but also determine how you can incorporate collaboration to enhance the outcome. This could mean doing the initial research yourself but seeking feedback from others.

Strengthen Your Network

If you aim to collaborate more, reach out to people whose skills complement yours. Whether in business or your personal life, building strong relationships with others will support both your goals and theirs. Set a goal to network or have meaningful conversations with three people who could support your objectives.

Review and Adjust

After implementing these steps, review your progress weekly. Reflect on what worked, what didn't, and where you felt most empowered. Continue to fine-tune your approach, knowing that the balance between independence and collaboration is dynamic and will shift over time.

Chapter 5

Energy Management, Focus, and Risk Assessment

"Wolves have a deep understanding of the natural world. They know when to hunt, when to rest, and when to retreat" - Farley Mowat

Thorne's Calculated Retreat

The air was crisp, and the light of dawn had barely touched the horizon when Thorne stirred from his rest. Now fully grown, his sleek, muscular frame rippled beneath his thick silver fur as he stretched. The pack was already stirring, preparing for the day ahead. Thorne was no longer the curious, eager youngster learning at the side of the alpha male. He was now a skilled and experienced wolf, actively taking part in the hunts that ensured the survival of his family. And today, it seemed, was no different.

Hard-earned lessons had marked Thorne's journey to adulthood. He had learned that a wolf's strength was not in brute force alone but in energy conservation, focus, and risk assessment. Today, he would put those lessons to the test. The pack had trailed a herd of elk for two days, studying their every movement, waiting for the perfect moment to strike.

The alpha male moved to the front of the group, his sharp eyes scanning the herd in the distance. Thorne watched closely, sensing the shift in mood as the alpha's gaze fixed on a specific elk—an older male whose movements were slower, labored. It was the perfect target: weaker than the others but enough to feed the entire pack. The alpha glanced at Thorne, silently allowing him to take the lead.

Thorne felt the weight of responsibility settle on him, but it was not unfamiliar. He had led smaller hunts before, but this was different. This time, the entire pack would follow his lead. His mind sharpened with focus, and he quickly assessed the terrain. Open plains spread out before them—an advantage for the elk, whose long legs and strength could easily outmatch even the fastest wolf. But Thorne had learned the importance of patience. This hunt would be about endurance, not speed.

Wolves, Thorne knew, were built for long chases. Their stamina allowed them to outlast their prey, covering vast distances in pursuit. Still, energy conservation was vital. He signaled to the pack to spread out, forming a loose semicircle. Their goal was not to startle the elk too soon but to gradually guide it toward terrain that would favor them.

Thorne's eyes never left the herd. He had learned to focus on the most minor details. The elk they had chosen to target moved stiffly. It was likely injured, making it a prime candidate for the wolves. But Thorne also knew that in a herd, even the healthier animals could make a mistake—one misstep on uneven ground, one moment of panic, and they could become just as vulnerable as the weakest.

The pack moved as one, each wolf knowing their role without the need for commands. The young wolves, still learning, stayed to the rear, observing how the more experienced members darted and weaved, pushing the herd gently toward a patch of forested ground where the thick undergrowth would slow the elk down. Thorne felt his pulse quicken. He could almost feel the moment approaching when the chase would begin.

But then, something shifted. Thorne's ears pricked as he caught a faint sound—a low growl from one of the younger wolves. It wasn't directed at the elk but at something else. His sharp eyes darted toward the edge of the plain, and there, appearing from the tree line, was a second herd of elk, moving at a brisk pace. If they joined with the herd Thorne was tracking, the situation would change drastically. The combined number of the two herds can make it far more difficult to isolate an individual elk, and the risk of injury would increase tenfold. A single kick from a frightened elk could break a wolf's jaw.

Thorne quickly calculated the odds. His instincts told him that while the injured elk remained a workable target, the approaching herd posed too much of a risk. He had seen it before—a hunt that seemed to be going well, only to turn into chaos when circumstances changed unexpectedly. A wolf could lose more than just the hunt; they could lose their life.

He growled softly, signaling the pack to slow their advance. The alpha male, watching from a distance, seemed to sense the danger as well. Thorne's heart raced as he weighed his options. Could they outmaneuver the new herd? Was there enough time to finish the hunt before the herds merged?

It was a dangerous gamble, one that Thorne wasn't willing to take. He had learned that not every hunt was worth the risk. Sometimes, it was better to retreat, conserve energy, and wait for a better opportunity. He growled again, louder this time, and the pack responded at once, falling back. Thorne had made his decision.

With one final glance at the elk, Thorne turned and led the pack away from the herd. The younger wolves hesitated at first, unsure why the hunt had been called off. But the older wolves followed without question, trusting Thorne's judgment. The alpha male moved alongside Thorne; his gaze filled with approval. Thorne had made the right choice.

As they returned to the cover of the forest, Thorne felt a surge of pride. The hunt had not ended in a kill, but it had been a success nonetheless. He had protected his pack, conserving their energy for another day. There would be more hunts and more opportunities. And when the time was right, Thorne knew they would succeed.

Wolf Lessons for Professional and Personal Life

Parallel Journeys – Mark and Sarah

Mark leaned back in his office chair, staring at the quarterly report on his desk. As the CEO of a growing tech company, he was no stranger to pressure. But recently, the weight of his responsibilities has been heavier than usual. Their latest product launch had been delayed, and the board was pushing for results. Mark knew he had to manage the company's resources carefully in the months ahead. A single misstep could mean financial strain and, ultimately, loss of trust from investors. The stakes were high.

At the same time, across town, Sarah was going through her own struggle. As a mother of two young children and a full-time nurse, life had been overwhelming. Between her shifts at the hospital, the children's after-school activities, and her personal goals, Sarah felt drained. Every day seemed like a race against the clock, and her physical and emotional energy was wearing thin. Balancing the demands of work and family left her with little time for herself, and she knew something had to change.

Mark and Sarah's paths, though different, shared many similarities. Like the wolves in Thorne's pack, they both faced challenges that required energy management, focus, and risk assessment. In their respective worlds, these lessons were essential not just for survival but for thriving. The lessons learned in the wilderness could help them find balance and success in their lives, both professionally and personally.

Energy Management: Conserving Resources and Personal Energy

For Mark, conserving the company's resources was becoming a priority. His company has seen rapid growth over the past year, but with growth came higher costs. Salaries had risen, marketing expenses had ballooned, and the development of their new product had taken longer than expected. Mark had always been ambitious, pushing his team hard to meet deadlines and exceed expectations. But now, he realized that continuing at this pace could burn them out and deplete the company's financial reserves.

He remembered the lesson from Thorne's story about energy management during the hunt. Thorne had learned that wolves, though powerful, were endurance predators. They conserved their energy for the right moment, pacing themselves during long chases to outlast their prey. Mark recognized that his company needed a similar approach. They couldn't sprint toward every goal without considering the long-term consequences. He called a meeting with his leadership team and proposed a more measured pace for the next few months. They would focus on maintaining the core business and carefully managing cash flow, ensuring they had enough reserves to weather any storms that might come.

Meanwhile, Sarah had her own realization. The exhaustion she felt wasn't just physical—it was mental and emotional, too. She had been giving so much of herself to her family and job that she had little left for her well-being. Like Thorne during a hunt, she needed to learn how to pace herself. She began by setting aside time each morning for herself, even if it was just ten minutes of quiet reflection before the chaos of the day began. She started saying no to unnecessary commitments and focused on conserving her energy for what truly mattered: her family, her health, and her work.

Energy management became a cornerstone of success in Mark and Sarah's lives. By learning to conserve resources—whether financial, physical, or emotional—they positioned themselves to be stronger and more resilient in the long run. The lesson Thorne learned in the wilderness was just as applicable to their modern lives.

Focus: Identifying What Truly Matters

As Mark adjusted the company's strategy, another challenge loomed. He needed to decide where to allocate the company's limited resources. They had several projects in development, but not all of them could be prioritized. Mark knew that without a clear focus, they risked spreading themselves too thin. His team needed direction, and he had to ensure they were working on the projects that would deliver the most significant impact.

Mark thought back to how Thorne and his pack selected their prey. The wolves didn't chase after every animal they encountered. Instead, they focused on those that were weaker or in a vulnerable position. Thorne had learned to focus on what would bring the best results rather than expending energy on a target that would ultimately be out of reach.

With this in mind, Mark called another meeting with his team to reassess their priorities. Together, they identified the projects that aligned most with the company's long-term goals. The new product launch, though delayed, was still a top priority. However, a few other side projects were put on hold. This allowed the team to channel their energy and resources into the most critical tasks. The focus brought clarity to their work, and Mark felt confident that they were now on the right track.

On a personal level, Sarah was also learning the importance of focus. Her life had become a blur of activity—work, family obligations, and social commitments all competed for her attention. She needed to identify what truly mattered and prioritize it accordingly.

Sarah realized that she had been trying to do everything perfectly: be the best mom and the most dedicated nurse while still finding time for her friends and hobbies. But this constant juggling act was unsustainable. After some reflection, she decided to scale back on her social commitments and focus more on her immediate family. She also made a conscious decision to prioritize quality time with her children over striving for perfection in every area. This newfound focus brought a sense of peace and direction to her days. She wasn't trying to be everything to everyone—she was focusing on what mattered most to her.

Both Mark and Sarah had learned the same lesson from Thorne's story. In both business and life, it's crucial to focus on the correct targets. Without clarity, resources get wasted, and burnout becomes inevitable. By honing in on what truly mattered, they found a sense of purpose and direction.

Risk Assessment: Weighing the Costs in Business and Life

As Mark guided his company, a new opportunity arose. A potential investor had expressed interest in acquiring a minority stake in the company. The investment could provide a much-needed cash infusion, but it also came with risks. The investor's vision didn't fully align with Mark's, and he worried that accepting the deal might lead to a loss of control over the company's direction.

Mark thought again about Thorne's lessons, this time focusing on risk assessment. In the wild, wolves face danger every time they hunt. A single miscalculation—like a well-placed kick from an elk—could injure or kill a wolf. Thorne had learned to assess risks carefully, understanding that some hunts simply weren't worth the potential danger. Sometimes, the best decision was to retreat and wait for a better opportunity.

With this in mind, Mark took a cautious approach. He arranged multiple meetings with the potential investor, carefully weighing the benefits and risks of the partnership. He also consulted with his board and legal advisors, ensuring he had a complete understanding of the implications. In the end, he decided not to go ahead with the investment. The risks outweighed the rewards, and Mark was confident that his company could continue to grow without it. Like Thorne, he had chosen the path of caution, knowing that the right opportunity would come along in time.

Sarah, too, found herself facing a crucial decision in her personal life. She had been considering going back to school to further her nursing career, but the timing didn't feel right. Between her work schedule and the demands of raising her children, taking on the extra commitment seemed risky. She worried about the financial strain, the time away from her family, and the added stress.

Thorne's lesson in risk assessment resonated with Sarah. Just as the wolves weighed the risks before attacking their prey, she needed to carefully consider the impact of going back to school. After discussing it with her husband and considering her options, Sarah decided to wait. The risk of taking on too much at once was too significant, and she knew she needed to conserve her energy for her current priorities. The opportunity to further her education would still be there when the time was right.

For both Mark and Sarah, risk assessment played a crucial role in their decision-making processes. Thorne's story had taught them that wisdom lay in knowing when to take a risk and when to retreat.

The Interconnectedness of Work and Life

As the months passed, Mark's company stabilized, and Sarah found a better balance in her personal life. Though their challenges were different, the principles of energy management, focus, and risk assessment guided them both. They had learned to conserve their energy for the right moments, focus on what truly mattered, and assess risks with a clear mind.

The lessons they applied in one realm often carried over to the other. Mark noticed that as he became more focused and intentional in his business, he also found more clarity in his personal life. He spent more time with his family and learned to delegate responsibilities at work, trusting his team to handle the day-to-day operations. Sarah, on the other hand, found that the lessons she learned in managing her family's energy and priorities helped her become more efficient and effective at work. She had a clearer sense of what needed her attention and what didn't.

Both Mark and Sarah realized that their personal and professional lives were deeply intertwined. Success in one area often supported success in the other. The balance they had achieved wasn't perfect, but it was sustainable. They continued to draw on the lessons learned from Thorne's story as they navigated the complexities of modern life.

Whether hunting for prey in the wilderness or striving for success in the modern world, the same principles apply. Energy, focus, and risk are all part of the journey, and managing them well is the key to thriving.

Reflection

Imagine yourself standing in the quiet woods at dawn, the air filled with the promise of a new day. You are not alone—Thorne is beside you. His amber eyes meet yours, and though no words are exchanged, you understand. The journey you've been on together has led to this moment. You've learned much from him, but now, it's time to reflect.

"Tell me," Thorne begins, his voice low and steady, "how do you manage your energy? Are you pacing yourself, like we wolves do on long hunts, or are you running headlong without thought, burning out before you reach your goal?"

Take a moment. Consider how you expend your energy each day. Do you find yourself rushing from task to task, barely catching your breath, or do you reserve your strength for what truly matters? Think about your personal and professional life. Are you managing your resources wisely, or are you depleting them without realizing it? What could you do differently?

"Every wolf learns to conserve energy," Thorne continues, strolling through the trees. "We know when to sprint and when to hold back. A hunt is a marathon, not a sprint. The same is true for you."

Now, pause. In your life, whether it's a business challenge or a personal goal, how can you better conserve your energy? Picture a typical day. Are there activities or people that drain you unnecessarily? What could you cut back on to save energy for more important pursuits? Imagine yourself choosing to focus on fewer, higher-priority tasks. How would that feel?

"Let's talk about focus," Thorne says, his eyes narrowing as if spotting prey in the distance. "When you hunt, you must see what others miss. A pack can only thrive if it knows which prey to chase. And so, I ask you—do you know your target?"

Do you? Take a moment to reflect. In your business or personal life, are you clear on what matters most, or are you chasing everything at once? Picture yourself standing on the edge of a forest, scanning the horizon. What is your target? Have you chosen it carefully, or is it simply what's nearest or most convenient? What would happen if you focused all your energy on that one goal?

> "Be like a wolf; silently observe, adapt to the environment, and strike when the time is right"

"As wolves," Thorne continues, "we observe our prey for days, looking for weaknesses and opportunities. We don't act until we are certain. What about you? Are you focusing your attention where it matters, or are you distracted by things that won't bring success?"

Finally, Thorne pauses, looking directly at you. "And now, we must speak of risk. Every hunt carries danger. But not every risk is worth taking. Tell me—do you assess your risks wisely?"

Think about your life right now. What risks are you facing? Maybe it's a big business decision, or perhaps it's a change in your personal life. Imagine yourself standing at the crossroads, unsure of which path to take. One road looks more straightforward, but is it the right one? The other path is uncertain, but the rewards could be greater. What factors should you consider before you move forward? How do you measure the risks against the potential rewards?

"Wolves understand risk," Thorne says softly. "We know that a kick by a hoof or being gored by an antler can end us. So, we calculate. We weigh the cost of the hunt. You must do the same."

Now, picture a hypothetical scenario. You've been offered an opportunity that seems tempting, but something feels off. What do you do? Do you rush in, trusting your instincts, or do you pause and assess? What information do you need to make a smart decision? Remember, just as in the wild, sometimes it's wiser to retreat and wait for a better chance.

Thorne turns to you, his eyes softening. "The lessons you've learned here," he says, "are not just about survival. They are about thriving. Energy, focus, and risk—these are the foundations of your journey. How you apply them will define your success."

Take a deep breath and reflect once more. You've walked with Thorne through the wilderness of your own life. You've seen how the principles of the wolf pack apply to your world. The question now is: How will you carry these lessons forward?

Action Plan

Here are suggestions for implementing the chapter's lessons.

Manage Your Energy

Identify Priorities: Focus on high-impact tasks. Avoid unnecessary activities that drain your energy.

Pace Yourself: Break tasks into smaller steps to avoid burnout. Take breaks to recharge.

Set Boundaries: Learn to say no to commitments that don't align with your goals.

Sharpen Your Focus

Clarify Your Goals: Define what truly matters, both in your personal and professional life.

Eliminate Distractions: Identify what pulls your attention away and remove or minimize it.

Create Daily Focus Time: Set aside uninterrupted time to work on your most important tasks.

Assess Risks Wisely

Weigh Pros and Cons: Before making decisions, carefully evaluate the potential risks and rewards.

Gather Information: Make informed choices by researching and consulting trusted sources.

Know When to Pause: Sometimes, it's better to wait for a more favorable opportunity.

Recommended reading

To delve deeper into the topics of energy management and focus, consider reading *Mastering Time for Productivity: A Guide to Improve Efficiency in Work and Life* from the series (refer to Appendix B: Resources for the link).

Chapter 6
Conclusion

"The lion may be more powerful but the wolf does not
perform in the circus" – Unknown

Thorne's Ascension

Thorne stood at the head of the pack, his amber eyes scanning
the open plains ahead. The early morning light cast long
shadows, highlighting the strong and lean muscles that rippled
beneath his fur. Thorne was no longer the young wolf learning
the ways of the hunt. He was now in his prime, a seasoned leader
who had grown both in strength and wisdom. He had learned the

lessons of leadership from the alpha male, and now, he led with a quiet authority that commanded respect.

The pack was on the move again, their target a herd of elk grazing in the distance. Thorne's mind was focused, his senses sharp as he directed the wolves to form a wide arc, approaching the herd without alarming them. He had led many hunts before, but this time felt different. There was a sense of finality in the air as if the pack itself understood that change was coming.

The alpha male, who had guided the pack for years, moved more slowly now. His once powerful strides were measured, his movements deliberate. Age had begun to weigh on him, but his eyes were still sharp, filled with the wisdom of years spent leading the pack. Thorne had noticed this shift, the gradual decline in the alpha's physical strength, and he knew the time for change had arrived. Yet, there was no aggression in the air, no need for a challenge or display of dominance. The alpha had taught Thorne everything he knew, and now, silently, he was ready to pass the mantle of leadership to his prodigy.

As the pack advanced, Thorne paused and glanced back at the alpha. Their eyes met, and at that moment, there was an unspoken understanding between them. The alpha had been watching Thorne closely over the past few months, observing how he handled the responsibilities of leadership. He had seen Thorne grow from an eager hunter into a wolf capable of making the tough decisions that came with leading a pack. And now, with quiet pride, he knew the pack was safe.

Peaceful transitions in wolf packs were not the norm. In many cases, challenges to the alpha's status could lead to fierce confrontations and sometimes violence. But there were exceptions. A pack as strong and cohesive as this one could navigate such changes without bloodshed. The alpha, though still respected and revered, had chosen to step aside. There would be no battle, no show of dominance. Instead, he would pass the torch willingly, knowing that Thorne was ready.

As Thorne turned back to face the pack, the moment felt heavy with emotion. The wolves behind him sensed the shift as well, their movements slowing as they waited for Thorne's following command. He took a deep breath and lifted his head, signaling the pack to advance. They moved as one, following his lead without hesitation. Thorne's heart swelled with pride, not just for his leadership but for the strength of the pack as a whole. Each wolf played their role with precision, working together in perfect harmony. They were more than just a group of hunters—they were a family.

The alpha male watched from the rear, his eyes never leaving Thorne. He no longer needed to be at the front of the pack. His time leading the hunts had ended, but his role was far from over. In stepping aside, he had not lost his place within the pack; he had simply evolved. He would remain a respected elder, his wisdom guiding the pack through challenging times, even if his body could no longer lead the way.

As the hunt progressed, the pack's movements grew more fluid, more unified under Thorne's direction. The elk herd was unaware of their presence until it was too late. With a final signal from Thorne, the wolves surged forward, closing in on their prey. The chase was long but efficient, a testament to Thorne's skill as a leader. The pack brought down the elk, and as they gathered around their meal, there was a palpable sense of celebration in the air. Thorne had led them well, and the hunt had been a success.

But as the pack fed, Thorne's thoughts drifted back to the alpha male. He glanced over and saw the elder wolf standing a little apart from the others, watching with quiet satisfaction. There was no regret in the alpha's eyes, only pride. He had done what every great leader must eventually do—he had prepared the next generation to take his place. And now, as Thorne stood at the head of the pack, the alpha could step back, knowing that the wolves would thrive under new leadership.

Thorne had proven himself not just through his strength but also through his wisdom and his care for the pack. The transition was complete, and the pack, once again, stood united.

The lesson of the wolf pack was clear. Leadership was not about dominance or control—it was about service, wisdom, and knowing when to step aside for the good of the whole. Thorne had learned this from the alpha, and now, he carried that lesson with him. The pack would continue to thrive, not because of one wolf's power but because of the strength they found in each other.

Recap

In this journey, we've followed Thorne's growth from a curious wolf pup to a skilled leader, drawing powerful lessons about leadership, resilience, communication, and collaboration. These themes are woven into the narrative of Thorne's development and serve as critical insights for anyone seeking to apply the wisdom of the wolf to their own life and work. Let's take a moment to recap the central lessons from each chapter, focusing on the core themes without repeating familiar details.

Chapter 1, *The Pack Mentality – Leadership Hierarchy and Teamwork*, introduced the essential dynamics of leadership and teamwork. Thorne began his journey by observing the pack's hierarchy, where the alpha male leads through wisdom, not force. This insight teaches us that authentic leadership is not about physical dominance but rather about earning respect and guiding others with confidence. Thorne's initial steps in understanding how every wolf has a role within the pack became the foundation of his growth. In a business or family setting, this translates to understanding that each person has a unique contribution, and collective success is achieved when individuals work together toward a shared goal. The lesson here is clear: influential leaders empower their teams by fostering collaboration and allowing every member to shine in their respective roles.

Chapter 2, *Adaptability, Resilience, and Resourcefulness*, takes us through the harsh realities of Thorne's first winter. The once bountiful summer had passed, leaving the pack facing a season of scarcity and cold. Thorne had to learn quickly that survival in these conditions required not just strength but adaptability. The lessons of resilience became apparent as the pack struggled with hunger and the unforgiving winter landscape. Thorne observed how the wolves adjusted their hunting techniques, shifting from chasing fast prey to scavenging for whatever was available. The resourcefulness they displayed showed that success isn't just about thriving in ideal conditions but about adapting to the challenges of a changing environment. In life, this means learning to pivot when faced with difficulties and finding ways to overcome obstacles, even when the odds are against us. Resilience is the key to enduring and thriving during tough times.

In **Chapter 3**, *Communication and Social Bonds*, Thorne experienced one of the most critical lessons of his journey—how wolves communicate and form deep social bonds. His first howl symbolized his growing connection to the pack and the power of collective voice. The howling was more than just noise; it was a form of communication that could travel across vast distances, helping wolves find one another when separated. Through this, Thorne learned that communication within the pack was essential for maintaining unity. The bonds between the wolves were strengthened by this ongoing exchange, whether through howling or more subtle forms of interaction. This chapter underscores the importance of communication in building solid teams and personal relationships. In business or family life, transparent and open communication is the foundation of trust and collaboration, allowing us to express needs, resolve conflicts, and strengthen our connections with others.

Chapter 4, *Independence and Collaboration*, explored the delicate balance between standing on one's own and working together. Thorne ventured out alone for the first time, testing his ability to survive without the pack's support. His first struggles taught him valuable lessons in independence—learning to hunt on his own and navigate the dangers of the wilderness. However, as time passed, Thorne realized that true strength didn't lie in isolation. The challenges of solo survival showed him the limitations of independence, and he longed to return to the pack. When he did return, Thorne fully understood the power of collaboration. He was a stronger wolf for having ventured out on his own, but he was even stronger when working as part of the pack. In our own lives, there is a time for independence and a time for collaboration. Both are necessary for growth, but we achieve the most when we find a balance between the two, leveraging the support and strengths of others while maintaining our capabilities.

"A wolf doesn't concern himself with the opinions of sheep"

Finally, **Chapter 5**, *Energy Management, Focus, and Risk Assessment*, brought Thorne's journey to a place of wisdom and strategic thinking. Now a fully grown wolf, Thorne led some of the pack's hunts, but his approach was different from when he was younger. He had learned to conserve his energy, focus on the most critical targets, and carefully assess risks before making decisions. These lessons came into sharp focus during a hunt where Thorne had to weigh the costs of pressing forward versus retreating. He decided to step back, understanding that not every opportunity was worth the risk. This moment highlighted the importance of making thoughtful decisions, especially when the stakes are high. In both business and personal life, the ability to manage energy and assess risks is crucial for long-term success. Rushing into decisions without considering the potential costs can lead to failure, but careful planning and patience often lead to better outcomes.

Throughout these chapters, the central themes of leadership, adaptability, communication, collaboration, and strategic thinking are woven into Thorne's story. His journey from a young, curious pup to a wise and capable leader mirrors the path we all must take in our own lives. Whether we are leading teams, managing family responsibilities, or navigating personal growth, the lessons learned from the wolves offer valuable guidance. By reflecting on these themes, we can apply them to our own challenges and find the strength, wisdom, and unity needed to thrive.

Final Words of Encouragement

As you reach the end of this journey, it's essential to reflect on the lessons we've uncovered. You, like Thorne, have the power to adapt, lead, and thrive. Life presents challenges, and in those moments, the choices you make determine the strength and clarity with which you move forward. Each step, no matter how small, brings you closer to the life and success you aim to achieve.

Remember that leadership starts with understanding yourself. Whether you're guiding a team or navigating personal growth, your actions set the tone for everything else. Authentic leadership is not about control but about inspiration. You don't need to have all the answers, but you must be willing to listen, learn, and guide others with empathy and purpose.

Resilience is one of the greatest strengths you can develop. The road to success is rarely smooth, but your ability to adapt and persevere will carry you through the most challenging times. Even when it seems like things are working against you, take a breath, assess the situation, and keep going. Trust in your ability to find solutions and overcome obstacles.

Finally, remember the importance of balance. It's easy to get caught up in the rush of life, chasing one goal after another. But true success is about finding harmony between work and life, independence and collaboration, effort and rest. Taking the time to recharge, reflect, and reconnect with what matters most will make all the difference.

You have everything you need within you to succeed. Trust in your journey, keep learning and know that with focus and perseverance, you will continue to thrive.

Thank you for reading!

If you found this book helpful, I'd greatly appreciate it if you could take a moment to leave a review on Amazon. Your feedback not only helps me improve but also assists other readers in finding the right resources. Scan the QR code (or click on it) to share your thoughts.

I appreciate your support!

Appendix A: Action Plan

All resources can be downloaded from our website, visit www.impisimedia.com/resources. You'll need to register for a free account and enter the access code to unlock the materials. **Access Code: WEDGE**

Chapter 1:

Business Culture with a Handbook

Create a concise hymn sheet outlining your company's vision, mission, values, and beliefs. Make sure these principles are clear, actionable, and relatable to all employees. Distribute the document and hold regular discussions with your team to ensure alignment. Lead by example by embodying these values in your daily decisions and interactions. Reinforce the culture by recognizing employees who model the company's values and consistently refer to the hymn sheet when addressing issues or making strategic decisions.

Refer to Appendix B: Resources – Hymn sheet template.

Family Culture with Guiding Values

Develop a set of guiding values for your family. These should be simple and easy to understand for all family members, regardless of age. Post these values in a visible place and explain their importance. Lead by example by living these values every day, ensuring that your actions align with the principles you've set. When conflicts arise, remind family members of shared values and reinforce positive behaviors by acknowledging them.

Refer to Appendix B: Resources – Family values template.

Chapter 2

Taking the lessons of adaptability and resilience into your daily life requires intentional action. Here is a simple, actionable plan you can implement.

Identify Challenges

Make a habit of regularly identifying both personal and professional challenges. Being aware of your challenges is the first step.

Evaluate Your Response

After identifying a challenge, reflect on how you typically respond. Do you resist change, or do you adapt? Be honest with yourself and think about how you could improve your response to future obstacles.

Develop Adaptability Skills

Train yourself to be more adaptable by actively seeking opportunities to embrace change. Start small—try a novel approach to an old task or embrace modern technology. Building adaptability in small ways will prepare you for more significant shifts.

Build Resilience

Focus on building resilience over time. This could involve improving your critical thinking skills, developing a more robust support network, or setting small, achievable goals that foster perseverance.

Reflect and Adjust

Set time aside every week to reflect on your progress. How have you adapted? What have you learned? Use this reflection to adjust your strategies and continually improve.

Chapter 3

Here are suggestions for improving communication and social bonds.

Listening

The next time you're in a conversation, make a conscious effort to focus solely on what the other person is saying. Avoid interrupting, and instead, ask open-ended questions to show your interest. Try this for a week and reflect on how it changes your communication dynamic.

Speaking

Before you speak, especially in difficult conversations, pause to consider the outcome you hope to achieve. What message do you want to convey? Practicing this mindfulness before speaking can help ensure that your words align with your intentions.

Bonding

If you're part of a team, family, or social group, consider implementing regular check-ins. This could be a daily five-minute meeting at work to update everyone on key issues or a weekly one-on-one with a partner to discuss feelings, goals, and concerns. Regular, honest communication fosters a sense of belonging and keeps relationships strong.

Foster trust

To build trust, be transparent in your communication. If you're uncertain about something, express that uncertainty instead of pretending to have all the answers. Being honest, even when it's uncomfortable, creates a foundation of trust that strengthens every relationship.

Adapt

Reflect on the different people you communicate with daily. Are you adapting your communication style to suit each situation, or are you using the same approach in all settings? Try to adjust how you communicate depending on the needs and preferences of the person you're interacting with.

Chapter 4

Here are suggestions for finding your balance between independence and collaboration.

Assess Your Current Situation

Identify whether you're currently leaning more towards independence or collaboration in your personal and professional life. Write down two situations where you acted independently and two where you collaborated with others. Reflect on the outcomes of each.

Define Your Goals

Decide on an area where you want to grow—whether it's improving your self-reliance or fostering better teamwork. Create a short-term goal that emphasizes the area you need to develop. For example, if you want to strengthen your independence, set a goal to take on a solo project. If you want to work on collaboration, seek out a partnership or group project.

Find Your Balance

Commit to blending independence and collaboration. Identify one task or challenge on which you can work independently, but also determine how you can incorporate collaboration to enhance the outcome. This could mean doing the initial research yourself but seeking feedback from others.

Strengthen Your Network

If you aim to collaborate more, reach out to people whose skills complement yours. Whether in business or your personal life, building strong relationships with others will support both your goals and theirs. Set a goal to network or have meaningful conversations with three people who could support your objectives.

Review and Adjust

After implementing these steps, review your progress weekly. Reflect on what worked, what didn't, and where you felt most empowered. Continue to fine-tune your approach, knowing that the balance between independence and collaboration is dynamic and will shift over time.

Chapter 5

Here are suggestions for implementing the chapter's lessons.

Manage Your Energy

Identify Priorities: Focus on high-impact tasks. Avoid unnecessary activities that drain your energy.

Pace Yourself: Break tasks into smaller steps to avoid burnout. Take breaks to recharge.

Set Boundaries: Learn to say no to commitments that don't align with your goals.

Sharpen Your Focus

Clarify Your Goals: Define what truly matters, both in your personal and professional life.

Eliminate Distractions: Identify what pulls your attention away and remove or minimize it.

Create Daily Focus Time: Set aside uninterrupted time to work on your most important tasks.

Assess Risks Wisely

Weigh Pros and Cons: Before making decisions, carefully evaluate the potential risks and rewards.

Gather Information: Make informed choices by researching and consulting trusted sources.

Know When to Pause: Sometimes, it's better to wait for a more favorable opportunity.

Recommended reading

To delve deeper into the topics of energy management and focus, consider reading *Mastering Time for Productivity: A Guide to Improve Efficiency in Work and Life* from the series (refer to Appendix B: Resources for the link).

Appendix B: Resources

All resources can be downloaded from our website, visit www.impisimedia.com/resources. You'll need to register for a free account and enter the access code to unlock the materials. **Access Code: WEDGE**

1: Hymn Sheet Template

Company communications (hymn sheet template)

1. Market Environment and Core Problem

Guidance: Describe the current market landscape in which your business operates. Focus on the primary problem your target clients face, and how your company's offerings provide a solution. Keep it concise and focus on the relevance of the problem to your target audience.

2. Products and/or Services

Guidance: Provide a concise summary of the products or services your business offers. Focus on the essentials—what you sell. Detailed descriptions can follow later, in paragraph 10, so keep this high-level and easy to understand.

3. Unique Selling Point (USP)

Guidance: What sets your business apart from competitors? Describe your unique approach, innovation, or standout feature that makes your product or service different. Focus on the value that this uniqueness delivers to your clients.

4. Market Positioning (Elevator Pitch)

Guidance: This is your quick, memorable response to the question, "What do you do?" Prepare three versions of your elevator pitch:

- **Short** (10-15 words): For brief introductions.

- **Medium** (20-50 words): For when you have a little more time.

- **Long** (up to 75 words): For slightly more in-depth explanations. Keep it clear, concise, and focused on your value proposition.

5. Vision

Guidance: Your vision is aspirational—it is where the company ultimately wants to go, even if it may never be fully achieved. It should inspire and guide long-term direction. Keep it broad and motivating.

6. Mission

Guidance: This explains what your company does every day to move toward the vision. It's your company's purpose in action. Focus on what your employees work toward daily and how that aligns with solving client problems or delivering value.

7. Core Values

Guidance: List 4 or 5 key values that guide your company's behavior and decision-making. For each value, include a brief explanation. Keep the descriptions practical, explaining how each value affects daily operations and the client experience.

8. Business Principles

Guidance: These are the guiding principles that influence your business decisions and actions. They should reflect your company's priorities and how you manage challenges, opportunities, and ethical considerations. Keep them actionable and clear.

9. Why Us?

Guidance: Explain why clients should choose you over your competition. Focus on your competitive advantages, such as better service, unique expertise, or a specific problem you solve that others do not. Be clear about the tangible value you offer.

10. Detailed Value Offering

Guidance: Here, you can expand on the product or service descriptions you provided earlier. Focus on the details of how your offerings solve client problems or improve their experience. Avoid getting too technical; instead, highlight the key benefits your clients care about most.

General Tips: Keep each section straightforward and easy to read. Aim for clarity over complexity and ensure that the language resonates with both internal teams and external stakeholders. This template should serve as a quick reference point that helps everyone "sing from the same hymn sheet."

EXAMPLE: ABC Company communications

1. Market Environment and Core Problem

Small and medium-sized businesses often struggle with digital transformation. Many lack the technical ability to adopt cloud-based solutions that could boost efficiency and reduce costs. ABC Company addresses this gap by offering tailored digital solutions for businesses looking to modernize.

2. Products and/or Services

ABC Company provides cloud-based software solutions, IT consulting, and ongoing technical support. We specialize in implementing customizable platforms that help businesses improve their workflows and data management.

3. Unique Selling Point (USP)

Our unique approach combines comprehensive IT consulting with personalized cloud-based solutions. Unlike other providers, we focus on small to mid-sized businesses and offer customizable packages tailored to individual business needs.

4. Market Positioning (Elevator Pitch)

- Short: We help businesses streamline operations through personalized cloud-based solutions.

- Medium: ABC Company offers customizable cloud solutions and IT consulting to help small and medium-sized businesses improve efficiency and reduce costs.

- Long: ABC Company specializes in personalized cloud solutions for small and medium-sized businesses. We combine IT consulting with tailored software platforms that help companies manage their workflows more efficiently, cut costs, and stay ahead of competitors.

5. Vision

To empower every small and medium-sized business to achieve digital transformation and operate with the same efficiency as large corporations.

6. Mission

We provide customized cloud solutions and expert IT consulting to help businesses thrive in a digital world. Our mission is to simplify technology adoption for our clients, enabling them to focus on growing their core business.

7. Values

- **Innovation**: We embrace innovative technology to provide the best solutions for our clients.

- **Client-Centric**: Our clients' success is our top priority, and we are committed to helping them achieve their goals.

- **Integrity**: We operate with transparency, honesty, and an intense sense of ethics.

- **Collaboration**: We believe in teamwork, both within our company and with our clients.

- **Excellence**: We strive for excellence in every solution we deliver.

8. Business Principles

- **Client Success**: We prioritize the long-term success of our clients by delivering solutions that align with their business goals, ensuring continuous support and innovation to help them grow.

Employee Empowerment: We foster a culture of learning, collaboration, and growth within our team, ensuring that every employee feels valued and empowered to contribute to our shared success.

- **Community Engagement**: We actively take part in and give back to the communities in which we live and work, believing that strong, healthy communities are the foundation for sustainable business success.

- **Environmental Responsibility**: We are committed to minimizing our environmental footprint by adopting sustainable practices in our operations and encouraging our clients to do the same through eco-friendly digital solutions.

- **Innovation and Excellence**: We continuously seek new ways to improve our products and services, driving innovation and maintaining excellence in everything we do.

9. Why Us?

Clients choose ABC Company because we offer customized cloud solutions that meet the specific needs of small and medium-sized businesses. We provide ongoing IT support and ensure seamless integration of modern technologies.

Our focus on personalized service, combined with our expertise in digital transformation, sets us apart from other providers.

10. Detailed Value Offering

At ABC Company, we deliver a range of cloud-based solutions that include data management, workflow automation, and secure IT infrastructure. Our expert consultants collaborate with each client to understand their unique challenges and design solutions that increase efficiency and reduce costs. We also provide ongoing support to ensure that clients maximize the value of their technology investments.

2. Family Values Template

Our family values

Honesty

We are always honest in what we say or do.

Kindness

We are always kind to others—people and animals.

Neatness

We always clean up after we've messed up.

Friendliness

We always greet everybody when we arrive or depart.

3. Recommended Reading

 To delve deeper into the topics of energy management and focus, consider reading **_Mastering Time for Productivity: A Guide to Improve Efficiency in Work and Life_** from the Smart Work-Life series.

4. Recommended Viewing

 Click or scan this QR code to watch a video of wolf howls.

About the Author

Ellen Sedge is a seasoned entrepreneur with a career that has evolved from mastering financial systems to helping other entrepreneurs. With a background that spans from simple bookkeeping to advanced financial systems, Ellen founded a training academy early in her career and later served as an independent consultant for medium-sized businesses. Seeking a better work-life balance, she transitioned to a home-based business, selling personal care products, and later launched two other businesses in another country. As an avid reader and keen traveler, Ellen has visited countries on five continents, enriching her perspective.

Her firsthand experience in time management and discipline, gained from working independently, provides valuable insights to entrepreneurs in the small business sector and digital nomads alike. Ellen's passion lies in empowering others to navigate the challenges of entrepreneurship with confidence and skill.

About the Publisher

Impisi™ Media is a dynamic publishing company dedicated to creating and distributing high-quality intellectual property, including books, e-books, audiobooks, and journals.

Our content is crafted to inform, inspire, and empower a global audience. Our commitment to innovation and excellence drives us to deliver content that resonates and adds value to our readers and listeners.

Visit our website https://impisimedia.com

f facebook.com/impisimedia

⧉ instagram.com/impisimedia

𝓟 pinterest.com/impisimedia

www.ingramcontent.com/pod-product-compliance
Lightning Source LLC
Chambersburg PA
CBHW071200120626
46546CB00006B/2348